About the Author

Michelle Brown was born and raised in a dysfunctional family and persevered through adverse circumstances. As an adult, she became resilient in finding peace and love within her soul, only when she went through a spiritual awakening. Tapping into her psychic abilities that emerged and surrendering to the universe allowed the faith within her to conquer obstacles and challenges during the transformation. Following all the universe's signs and messages, she has written this first book and found her way home.

Blindsided: My Spiritual Journey to Love Oneself

Michelle Brown

Blindsided: My Spiritual Journey to Love Oneself

Olympia Publishers
London

www.olympiapublishers.com
OLYMPIA PAPERBACK EDITION

Copyright © Michelle Brown 2024

The right of Michelle Brown to be identified as author of
this work has been asserted in accordance with sections 77 and 78 of
the Copyright, Designs and Patents Act 1988.

All Rights Reserved

No reproduction, copy or transmission of this publication
may be made without written permission.
No paragraph of this publication may be reproduced,
copied or transmitted save with the written permission of the publisher,
or in accordance with the provisions
of the Copyright Act 1956 (as amended).

Any person who commits any unauthorized act in relation to
this publication may be liable to criminal
prosecution and civil claims for damage.

A CIP catalogue record for this title is
available from the British Library.

ISBN: 978-1-80439-970-5

This book is memoir. It reflects the author's present recollections of experiences over time. Some names and characteristics have been changed, some events have been compressed, and some dialogue has been recreated.

First Published in 2024

Olympia Publishers
Tallis House
2 Tallis Street
London
EC4Y 0AB

Printed in Great Britain

Acknowledgments

Thank you to my mom, for all the love and support she has shown throughout the process of writing this book. I appreciate her vulnerability in providing very personal information, so I can fulfill my soul's growth; to inspire and guide others during their spiritual transformation.

Coming into the World of Dysfunction

My Mom's Path of Life

Did you ever look at a road map and wonder which way to go? Well, that is what the family tree I was born into turned out to be. Statistics show that three in ten teen American girls will get pregnant at least once before age twenty. My mom was one of those statistics. She got pregnant at the age of sixteen.

My mom was absolutely stunning, with thick shoulder-length auburn-colored hair, piercing green eyes, and a thin build that any girl would die for. She resembled a younger version of Audrey Hepburn. In the 1960s, if you were a pregnant high school teen, the school board would make you drop out. My mom never gave them the chance, she up and quit. After quitting high school, my mom's parents made her get married instantly to the father. Since she was so young, her parents had to sign off on the marriage certificate. Even though they were newlyweds, they both lived in two different homes with their parents. Being forced to get married at such a young age and living separate lives, the divorce took place less than a year of marriage. My older sister Colleen was born, with no father in sight. He gave up all his rights, and now as a single mother, she knew she had to find employment. But who was going to hire her without a high school diploma? It took a while, until she found a small diner that hired her as a waitress. As time went on working at the diner, her life seemed to be going in the right direction. She was interested in dating again and decided to take night courses to complete her high school diploma. She then accomplished what she thought was inevitable, obtaining a high school diploma as a single mom. Working at a small diner, you get to know the regular patrons. One customer that really caught her eye was a charming young man dressed in an Army National Guard uniform. He had blonde hair with bright blue eyes and very petite. The only item he ordered on the menu was coffee. He came in pretty frequently, as he also delivered fresh loaves of bread to people's homes. As his waitress, they grew on each other. She always said it wasn't love at first sight; it was the uniform that caught her eye. He was twenty-one when they met. He was also going through a divorce and had a daughter, which he had given up his rights to. Being young and dumb, as she would say, she married him on Aug 21, 1965.

Inner Child Shattered

My Arrival from the Womb with Attitude

You know how in movies or magazines we've all seen the tender clips of the pregnant mom putting headphones around their belly so the baby can listen to music? Unfortunately, my mom didn't give me that luxury; all I heard was the fighting and screaming. So, I came out of her womb screaming with an attitude. I have heard many horror stories about couples who married and only then, the true self comes out. That became the situation among my parents. After they married, my mom realized that this man, my dad, was really an alcoholic, abusive, and narcissistic being.

It was a warm, dark summer night at 12.15 a.m., when I was born, Aug 31, 1968. They were expecting a boy and planned on naming me Michael. Surprise! I wasn't born with those body parts so they changed my birth name to Michelle. My birth was only one day after my dad's legal adoption was finalized with Colleen. I was not a happy camper when I emerged here in this world. You could see the "What the hell, put me back in the womb!" expression from my wide-opened, sapphire-shaded eyes. They reflected the color of the sea. Not only were my eyes wide open, but then I think the whole city of Harrisburg, PA, heard me screech. I weighed six pounds four ounces with a set of lungs and thick jet-black hair spiking straight up and entirely all over my head, as if I put my finger in an electric socket. The nurses cleaned me up, tried to comb my hair downwards to look somewhat presentable for the baby pictures the staff took in the hospital. But it was next to impossible, as my hair had a mind of its own. At least, I stopped screaming long enough for them to take the picture.

In the 1960s, new moms were able to stay in the hospital for a week. After being released from the hospital, my parents took me home to a two-bedroom apartment on 13 Street in Harrisburg. It was located on the second floor of an old, brick, three-story apartment complex, that wasn't kept up very well. The wood around the windows were so rotted that whenever the wind blew, so did the curtains. The owner turned off the heat at nine p.m. every night to save on oil and turned it back on at six a.m. Colleen had her own room, and they put my crib in their room. At the age of twenty-two, this was the only housing they could afford with two children and only one parent working. My dad had the same occupation, delivering home-made loaves of bread to people's homes.

The first year of existence, I was on time with all my motor skills, the body weight and growth was just a tad under on the chart, as I was very petite. My mom and doctors only concern was my social skills. I was not performing like a normal happy baby. I never laughed, held in reserve, apprehensive (only wanted Mom) and wouldn't chatter. If the doctor knew what was really going on behind closed doors, at that moment he would understand completely.

By means of our family developing, therefore, the abuse heightened toward my mom. It began through verbal abuse. Nothing my mom did stood good enough; constantly degrading her, saying she's overweight, disliked her outfits and scolded her if she bought groceries that weren't necessary—in his eyes, anyway. His drinking became progressively worse. Alcohol and him didn't mix very well, as he became Dr. Jekyll and Mr. Hyde whenever he consumed multiple alcoholic beverages. When the drinking became excessively, that's when the physical abuse began. My mom became a hermit crab and wanted to stay out of the public eye; due to the embarrassment, my dad would create while being an abusive drunk. He could never stop with one alcoholic beverage, as he enjoyed being inebriated and would close the bars. Although, one evening my dad decided to take my mom on a date, which rarely happened. Hesitantly, she agreed. He made reservations at one of her favorite restaurants. While they were sitting at their table engaging in conversation, my dad noticed a young man glaring over at her. I'm pretty certain a lot of men would notice my mom because she's absolutely gorgeous. My dad's attitude switched and gave her the silent treatment during dinner. What was supposed to be a nice evening, just the two of them; triggered my dad into a monster and the torture began. He verbally abused her until they arrived home and then punched her in the face, expressing that she provoked it. This was just the glimpse of hell she started to live. My mom came from a very strict, non-affectionate family, but never experienced this type of abuse. It wasn't what she wanted nor asked for, so she decided to leave him. One day when my dad was working, she ran all through the house looking for money. Some was stashed in between mattresses (they didn't use banks), my dad's dirty jeans, and gathered any change that was lying around. Found just enough that when she went out looking for a new home. She found one and leased a little apartment. I was still a baby at the time, when she packed up all our belongings and took Colleen, and I to our new home on Shell Street. It wasn't the safest area in Harrisburg to raise children. There was a lot of crime, but then again, this apartment was all she could afford last minute.

Being a single parent with a baby and a five-year old, Mom had to find employment. She landed one at Berg Electronics, making computer parts. She hired a teenager that lived in the same apartment complex to babysit while she worked. Unfortunately, the salary she made wasn't enough to pay the monthly bills, and my dad wouldn't offer child or spousal support. He was agitated because she left, but kept fighting for our return. Her self-esteem was already low from being in an abusive relationship; but now, she became depressed, terrified, and embarrassed because she felt like a failure not being able to survive on her own with two small children. On rare occasions, Dad could be charming, loving, and caring. Usually, when he gets what he wants or not drunk. As he knew she was struggling, he would sweet talk, visit the family, and make promises he couldn't keep. My dad pleaded with my mom if she came home, he would change his behavior. He almost sounded like a broken record, as he kept repeating himself and making guarantees that he wouldn't drink, touch, or diminish her. It was obviously all lies just to lure her back, like a predator on the prowl. By this time, she was at a loss, so she caved in, and they reunited.

My dad, definitely an epitome of a narcissistic jerk. I was bounced everywhere like a rag doll the first year of my life, as it wasn't the first time my mom left and took him back, as she proceeded on round II.

When my mom gathered our belongings for the second time, she rented a small ranch house in a cute town, called Hummelstown. It was a two-bedroom home located at the end of town. It had white siding, black trim around the windows, a small yard, and close by was an enormous creek surrounded by forest. There was also a restaurant located right across the street from our home. The house was kept up pretty well, unlike the last two apartments we resided. The location was in a suburban area, which my mom thought was safer than city living. Unfortunately, the estrangement of my parents didn't last very long, as my dad moved in a month or two later. Deep within her soul, she knew it wasn't the best decision, but her self-worth was still low, and the hopelessness never subsided. I guarantee, if she was aware of what would happen next, her decision would have changed immediately. For the reason, that ultimately, the abuse trickled down towards me.

Living a Nightmare on Elm Street

No infant, toddler, or child should see, hear, or feel the pain that I had experienced first-hand from an abusive parent. Nothing had changed like my dad always promised; it only got worse. As I was growing into a toddler, so was my personality. I was becoming a very stubborn, and defiant little girl.

After my dad moved back in, he ended up getting a job in construction, assembling bridges. He worked ten to twelve-hour days, then stopped at the VFW to get inebriated. My mom quit her job at Berg Electronics to be a stay-at-home mom.

I was two at the time, when I grew out of my crib, which I never stayed in. Therefore, my mom purchased a twin bed. By moving me into Colleen's room, along with this new twin bed, it was like a little child in a candy store. Jumping up and down on the mattress, grinning from ear to ear, as Mom would mention. She also said, "You noticed the wheels turning around inside my little head during the same time, freedom!" Only, that freedom had a price to pay. This would be the start of my inner child being shattered.

I'm sure it wasn't just freedom that I didn't sleep at night, it also had to be anxiety. Yes, only two years old and having anxiety. What child wouldn't after having to listen to all the screaming and yelling; starting from my mom's womb, to now hearing it every day. Not to mention; witnessing all the physical abuse.

Colleen was scared to death of our father and knew better to provoke him. Always did what she was advised, discreet and stayed out of trouble. That was definitely not me, even at two years old. Colleen recalls the first time, and definitely not my last, when my dad physically abused me. She remembers every detail, as it's embedded in her head forever. It was extremely traumatic to watch, and for me to endure. This one evening, Mom put us to bed for the night and my dad came home inebriated. I kept getting out of bed and running around, as if the sun arose. Mom marched through the entryway and gave several warnings. She also asked me, "Do you want your dad to come in and punish you?"

Of course, I didn't care, as I was a defiant little girl, so I went about my business running around and playing. Not two minutes later, the door flew open, I froze in mid-air, dropped whatever I was doing, and leaped into bed. Colleen said, his face looked so evil that she was afraid for my life. He took off his belt, grabbed me by the arm, and pulled me out of bed. He then, twirled me around and made me bend over. As he tore off my pajamas, the underwear came off too. When I was bending over naked, the belt came flying across my butt and back.

With every whistle and smack along my small, lean body, my sister would hide her face and cringe. She was seriously afraid for my life. As I cried and yelled during every belt slapping, he would hit me harder and say, "If you cry, I'll give you something to cry about!" I quit crying, pushed the pain away, so he would leave me alone. As soon as I did, he stopped hitting me. He told me to get dressed, and never get out of bed again! As he left the room, Colleen walked over to console me. I was in so much pain, I could barely move. She said my back and butt had so many welt marks that she lost count. There were also imprints of the belt buckle and blood everywhere. I must have looked like Jesus, when he was crucified on the cross.

Did I follow through with what my father instructed to stay in bed? Unequivocally not; therefore, my mom called the doctor and made an appointment to discuss the matter. I was turning three by this time, and I have no idea where my mom found a lunatic of a counselor to address this matter. For the reason, his advised method was insane and undeniably abusive. He should have lost his license regarding my case. My mom was deathly afraid of Dad, and what he is capable of doing, so she went along with the doctor's orders. I was strapped down to my bed with a harness every night to keep me out of trouble.

"What am I?" A patient in a psych ward at the age of three? My mom was hoping this method worked, so I wouldn't get punished like the previous time. I think it may have lasted a night or two, holding me down like a hostage till I wiggled out and almost strangled myself. Luckily, my mom heard all the commotion, ran into to the room and rescued me. Again, the therapist should have been locked up for that insane method! Now, my mom was dumbfounded on how to keep me safe from my dad. One evening, I was out of bed again, and she came up with an idea. Like a light bulb went off in her head. Every time I would get out of bed, I would have to stand in the corner, until I was tired. That way she could keep an eye on me, so my dad wouldn't whip my butt. As a toddler, standing in a corner must of, felt like years, but my mom said it was merely twenty minutes until I was tired enough to stay in bed. This punishment stuck around for quite some time as it was affective. A few weeks later, the abuse I endured came to a halt. No, he did not become religious or did a one eighty and changed his life around, but because we had to move in with my grandparents.

    Studies show that kids begin forming explicit childhood memories at around two years of age. I started remembering bits and pieces at age four. It was June 22, 1972; there was a torrential downpour from tropical storm Agnes that came through Pennsylvania. Since I was sick with asthma, Mom placed Colleen and I in the car, and drove through the pouring rain to the doctors. The doctor gave me a breathing treatment and prescribed some antibiotics. We proceeded to the pharmacy to pick up the prescription and then off to home. Our doctor's appointment and pharmacy visit consisted of an hour or two. After driving down the highway, we came upon the street we resided on, only to find the street, our home, the entire neighborhood, and the restaurant across the street under water. The creek located near our home crested due to the nineteen inches of rain that fell over a period of days from Tropical Storm Agnes. Viewing from the public road, it was a complete catastrophe. After Mom pulled the car over on the side of the highway, we all walked around in the rain, looking in disbelief, as all you could see were the rooftops of the buildings. Mom was in shock since we were only gone for a couple of hours. Not only was our house under water, so was my dad's car. He received a DUI a couple months prior and lost his license, so Mom had to drive him to work every morning. Gazing across the horizon, Mom was feeling all these mixed emotions. It would go from miserable, destitute, anxious, to being grateful since we were all safe and alive. After she was done pondering, she put us back into the car and drove us to my grandparents. Later that night, we found out that my dad was safe as well. A co-worker drove him to a bar and that's where he resided for the night, as it too was surrounded by water and couldn't leave.

This was one of the most horrific storms Pennsylvania ever had. It caused two billion in damages including sixty-eight thousand homes, three thousand businesses and forty-eight deaths.

Grandparents

My grandparents lived in a small trailer court not far from our flooded home. We would visit them quite often, so I was very familiar with the trailer court and the location of their home. They had a small black gate attached to a fence surrounding their pristine yard. My grandfather (AKA Pop-Pop) maintained the grass so well, that it felt like you were walking on a golf course. The color of their home trailer had different browns and tans intertwined with each other, also had a touch of off white in some areas to offset some of the neutral colors. Every time we would visit my grandparents, my grandfather would be out there waxing the siding until it sparkled in the sunlight, or he would be on top of the roof applying aluminum paint. The outside of their home always looked immaculate, and so was the inside. As you walk up a few wooden steps, there was a small landing which led you to the front door and into their living room. They had matching couch and chairs covered in plastic. My grandparents must have sensed us kids would be staying there for a while or they were preparing to keep them forever. Either way, it was way too uncomfortable to sit on. Their home wasn't overly decorated, and not many knickknacks. Family pictures were hung on the wall or placed on the end table. Behind the front door hung a huge homemade wooden paddle with holes and Billy Club. Yes, every time we came and visited, Pop-Pop presented it to us kids as a warning to stay out of trouble or else. I don't believe he ever used it on us children or my mom, but used it on her brothers. As you looked toward your left of the living room, there was a long narrow hallway that led to the two bedrooms and one bathroom. Then, if you look toward the right of the living room, there was their kitchen with a small, rectangular table that could possibly seat four people. They kept their home so clean you could eat off the floor. Not a speck of dust lying around. I guess, there's nothing else to do when you're retired but become OCD.

 I always dreaded going there for any length of time, but now we had to live there until we found a new home because of the flood. I was not a happy camper! It was like living with the Heat Miser, from the movie, *The Year Without a Santa Clause.* No toys allowed! Also, in their eyes, kids should be seen not heard. I had to go from almost four years old to an adult in a split second. My mom wasn't happy with the living conditions either, but there wasn't anything she could do. With the water that high, she had a gut feeling we literally lost everything, from photo albums, important documents like birth certificates, furniture, to my dad's vehicle. Some of our clothes and shoes might be salvageable but that would be it. I guess we could look on the bright side, the abuse stopped during the time we lived with my grandparents.

 The day after the flood, the sun was out and very humid. Summer months in Pennsylvania can be brutal with humidity. As we drove to our house to gather some belongings that may have been salvageable, you could see the devastation the flood did to the entire community. When we pulled up into the driveway, there was still murky water lying everywhere, including inside the home. Even at the age of four, I still remember walking into the house of disaster and feeling the sadness that my family endured as we nearly lost everything. We rummaged through each room one by one to see what was worth saving. It was mostly clothes and toys. I have no idea why my mom would want to save the toys since we weren't allowed to play with them while living at my grandparents' house. We had to sit there and be quiet like a mime. After cleaning out the house and throwing everything away, we drove back to my grandparent's home to live. There were five of us total in a small two-bedroom home. The sleeping arrangements were horrible. They only had a single bed in the spare room so there were bodies everywhere from the couch, to the floor, to one small bed. We must have looked like sardines in a can. The only good factor with this living arrangement, my dad rarely came home. He was either at the bar getting inebriated or working out of town building bridges.

The summer went by like a traveling snail. I was scared to death of my grandfather, (had no clue why, because I wasn't scared of my dad who beat me) and our grandmother always favored Colleen. My grandmother never hid her favoritism, as my mom can tell you first hand. Her brothers could do no wrong. Day after day, it was the same repetitive routine. Mom driving around town looking for a new place to live. I felt all alone, scared, and my childhood was taken from me. All I remember, while living there, was coloring in books or drawing at the kitchen table. Sometimes, I would go outside and walk around since they had a fenced-in yard. I didn't dare touch anything outside either, out of fear I would get the wooden paddle with holes on my butt. This lasted for three months, which felt like years, until my parents found a house under construction that would be ready to move in by September 1972.

New Childhood Home

My parents signed the mortgage papers, received the keys to the home, and were ready to move in! I was so excited, I felt like a little girl once more in a candy shop. Not to mention, my devilish side emerged. But, if I only knew what was going to happen next, I would have run away from home in a heartbeat. Living with my grandparents would have been heaven, rather than hell that I was going to endure.

This home was in a fairly new development, and the only thing surrounding it were cornfields and forests. Farmers sold the land to developers. Subsequently, it was in the middle of nowhere and nothing else was around. The house was in the same town we lived in before the flood; safe and the school district was ranked one of the best around the area.

The style of our new home was a small ranch with a two-car attached garage, on half acre lot. The land was flat without any trees. The home had a nice size bay window, perfect for the sunshine to sparkle through, brick front and yellow siding along the rest of the house. Small bushes were planted underneath each window and along the sidewalk to the front door. When you entered the main entrance, you stepped into the living room, where the bay window was located. The kitchen was off the living room, which was visible from the front door. After you bypass the living room and kitchen, there was a small hallway with three bedrooms and a full bathroom. Since the house was brand new, each room had white walls. The only color that was in the house were the appliances, which were yellow. Yellow siding and yellow appliances. I don't think there were too many colors to choose from since yellow, brown, and green were the colors of the '70s. The builders were right on target with allowing us to move in by September. We had to get all new furniture for each room. It felt like Christmas Day as the deliveries kept coming and going. The best part of relocating to our new home was having my own bedroom! Hell, why not I had to grow up at the age of four. All grown-ups should have their own room, right?

As we got settle in with our daily routines, my devilish side went into full swing and so did learned behavior. My mom was a stay-at home mom and Dad was still in construction building bridges. He traveled with his company and would be gone a couple weeks out of the month. If he wasn't traveling, he was at the VFW getting inebriated. By this time, he received his license, but still driving intoxicated. Some evenings, he would pass out at the bar; the bartender would call Mom and advise her that she needed to retrieve her husband. Whenever he walked through that front door intoxicated, I knew exactly what was going to happen. He was going to whip my bare behind with his belt because I was standing in a corner, as he knew the reason why; I wouldn't stay in bed. Sometimes, he would pick a fight with my mom and smack her too. I recollect one evening, I was sound asleep when I was awakened in the middle of the night from my parents fighting. I tiptoed down the hallway until I came upon the kitchen, from where the argument was coming from. I peered around the corner and witnessed my dad punching my mom. I was so terrified he was going to kill her!

Without even thinking of what might happen to me next, I yelled, "STOP HITTING MY MOM," at the top of my lungs. I think the whole neighborhood heard me. When he turned around, if looks could kill, I would have been dead; my mom picked up a frying pan and threw it at him along with some lids. My body spun around so quickly that my face sideswiped the corner of the wall when I went running back to my bedroom. During the entire night, I was scared to move, that I stayed in bed trembling till I fell asleep. I think the angels were watching over me, because that night, he didn't come after me. The next day, my dad had no recollection of what happened the night previously. A usual typical alcoholic. This was our normal family life. The only new normal that arose was my mom abusing me too. Although, she considered it as punishment.

I was still four but going on thirty (not by choice) when one night I didn't sleep (nothing new there), so I decided to fill the bathtub and make some tea on the stove. At four years old, I may have thought I was an adult, but my intellect proved otherwise. I forgot to turn off the water to the bathtub, which flooded the entire bathroom and melted the teapot to the stove which smoked enough for the fire alarms to go off. OOPS! It woke my mom up, and thank goodness, my dad was out of town, or was it? Either way, I still received a spanking. I wasn't shocked, even though it was my mom's first time punishing me. It seemed like an everyday occurrence. My mom had never used a leather belt with a buckle before, but used a wooden spoon. Either way, I have been accustomed to hard objects whipping my bare behind.

There's only one memory that I thought my mom was psychologically abusive, because I felt like a stray animal being tossed into a cage. I was close to five years old when my mom tried to prepare me for kindergarten. Making sure, I was using my manners and utensils consistently. One night during dinner, the family rules were sitting together at the dinner table, say our dinner prayer, and eat all the food that was served on our plate. This particular night, I had an attitude and wouldn't recite the prayer or use the utensils properly. My mom became angry and grabbed me by the arm, along with the full plate of food; and threw me into the bathroom. She cursed and advised me to stay here and eat, since I ignored the rules. Sitting on the bathroom floor weeping, I crawled into a small linen closet, (hoping she wouldn't locate my hopeless little body) cradling myself to sleep. I never ate dinner that night.

I was abused on so many different levels. First, it began as physical, then psychologically and eventually turned to sexual abuse. (Nearly seventy percent of all reported sexual assaults occur to children ages seventeen and under. One in four girls and one in six boys will be sexually abused before they turn eighteen years old… Family members also accounted for **twenty-three percent of those abusing children ages twelve to seventy**).

Terror Begins

I was only four years old when my nightmare began; as I encountered my first time of sexual abuse. My inner child was already shattered by all the physical and psychological abuse.

My dad was home for a while; since he didn't travel for work until another bridge needed constructed. Although, when he was in the area, the family considered him an absent Dad and husband. His world consisted of consuming alcoholic beverages at his favorite bar and infidelity. I have been advised that there is an estranged sister in the area from his infidelity.

This one evening, all of us were sleeping when my dad came stumbling through the front entry inebriated. I was sound asleep when I heard the bedroom door slowly open, so I froze. I was confused to why he was entering my bedroom, because I was behaving for a change. When he proceeded to walk over to my bed, I must have looked like a deer in headlights because he put his hand over my mouth and ordered me to stay quiet or he would kill me. I followed his instructions, as I was scared for my life.

He pulled down his pants along with his underwear, and crawled into my bed. I was horrified to what the outcome might be, but again, I didn't dare move or speak as he would kill me! When he was under my covers, he pulled down my pajamas until I was naked from the waist down. He then made an attempt to have sexual intercourse with my innocent petite body. Over several failed attempts, he appeared frustrated and stopped trying. As he was getting dressed, he complained that my vagina wasn't the same size as my mom, that's why the encounter was unsuccessful. When he started walking out of the bedroom, he turned around and gave me the same warning. Never say a word about what just transpired, or he'd kill me. My lips were sealed, never said a word. Once more, my angels must have been watching over me.

(Approximately, fifteen hundred women are killed each year by husbands or boyfriends. About two million men per year beat their partners, according to the FBI. There is no excuse for abuse.) Now, I know how my mom felt. Every time, they would get into a physical altercation, he would tell her the same thing. He would kill her if she ever tried to leave. I have no doubt, that he would kill me too.

<u>*Battling Wars of Disabilities Caused by Trauma*</u>

At the end of August 1973, I finally turned five years old and was able to go to kindergarten. I barely made the cut off because of my birthdate, August 31, and elementary school began the first week of September. My mom was never going to send me to kindergarten that year because she thought I was too immature. For some reason, last minute, she had a change of heart and thought it would be beneficial to learn how to socialize with other children. I was never around them since I didn't attend daycare and my mom never had friends with children my age. The only interaction I had was when my uncle would visit from out of town, because my cousins were around the same age as Colleen and I. Going to kindergarten, the teachers made sure we used our manners and to be kind to one another. But living inside the house of horror, I lacked all of above since my only childhood was taken from me. What you see is what you learn. The only thing I learned so far was how to fight, yell, put up a front and never cry.

This one incident, my mom was out selling Avon, and Colleen was babysitting. I wanted to watch something on television, and she wouldn't allow me. In my mind, she's wasn't the boss and made me angry. I dashed into the kitchen, pulled a chair over to the telephone, as I was too petite to reach it from the floor. I picked up the handset to dial my grandmother's phone number, but my sister tried to grab it from me. The fighting escaladed to the point that I slammed the handset on her wrist. She screamed out of pain; I dropped the phone, and she called my grandma. I didn't feel remorseful at the time, as Colleen would tell you; I was always nasty and hitting her. It completely generates from learned behavior.

Friendships Creating

After being in kindergarten, I started coming out of my cocoon and making friends. This one particular friend lived in my neighborhood. Her home was in the perfect location since it was next to the bus stop and only a block away from mine. The only downfall with this connection was her parents. They wouldn't allow her to play outside. Sometimes we go-carted in her back yard; otherwise, we played inside her home. Ultimately, our friendship diminished, since I loved being outside even in the winter months. There were other children in the neighborhood, but they were older than I was. Since my mom never protested, I considered them to be neighborly friends.

I was becoming a social butterfly, and not interested in school. Kindergarten was only a half day with half hour naps, laying on mats located on the cement floor. During this brief period in school, evidently, I wouldn't listen to the teacher since I was always getting into trouble. To this day, I myself, still remember her name and what she resembled. This schoolteacher jogged my memory of the Grinch who hated children, absolutely, not a pleasant one. I believe some teachers have a hard time relating to young children, and she was one of them. Possibly, the teacher was the reason I never wanted to listen or it was the attention span that was the culprit. Whichever one it was, I never wanted to finish my assignments. The report cards and parent teacher conferences proved deficiency plus non-interest in school. The grading scale in kindergarten was based on plus signs, a check mark and check minuses. I received mostly check minuses which indicated the need for improvement. I felt maybe Mom was correct, I was immature for kindergarten. Or my attention and learning disabilities had everything to do with my home living.

My mom became pregnant, (which was definitely a surprise pregnancy) and had very little patience with my stubbornness or she was nauseous from the pregnancy.

Under Mom's circumstances and my attitude, she did the best she could providing help and guidance throughout my kindergarten year. Regrettably, that wasn't enough, and the teacher insisted on holding me behind in kindergarten. The teacher may have had some valid points in regards to holding me back, because I recall struggling with coloring inside the lines or following simple directions; like standing in a straight line with my peers. It was very challenging going through kindergarten and having the teacher reprimand my inabilities in front of the classroom. I already felt like an outcast, but now being embarrassed, I just wanted to curl up in a ball and roll away. In my eyes, I couldn't do anything right, whether it was home or in school. Mom conflicted with the teacher's decision and scheduled a meeting with the principle. They came to an agreement and placed me in readiness first grade. Basically, it was an all-day kindergarten. I just started to spread my wings and fly, to be put back into my cocoon. The rest of the children located in the classroom departed onto first grade. Summertime came and my sister was born on June 13, 1974. My parents named her Doreen. She was almost six years younger, and I also became into an older sister. I never showed annoyance to having an infant in the family. I was in my own little world; all I cared about is playing outside along with shenanigans. My mom allowed me to have freedom at the age of six. She was certain the neighborhood we lived in seemed secure. Besides, Colleen was there to protect me. My mom didn't realize that big sis didn't watch over me, as I proceeded to accomplish whatever I wanted to, even in her presence. After the handset incident, I believe she was scared of me.

  The house had been eerily peaceful except for Doreen crying all the time. My dad's construction company placed him in Tioga County (it's about a three-hour drive in the middle of nowhere) for business. He would stay in a motel three weeks at a time. My mom suspected that he had a girlfriend in the area and would spend workweeks with her too. When he graced us with his presence, it was only for the weekend. I recall one day during the weekend; our daddy daughters outing wasn't to visit the zoo, instead, he took us to the VFW. One drink led to another, until we're there for hours while my mom was working, selling Avon. Our dad never skipped drinking at his favorite bar in order to watch us kids. I remember sitting on the bar stool, twirling around, acting like we're cool, drinking a coke at the bar top with our dad. Or we would ask for some change to put in the jukebox to play our favorite songs (more like Colleen's songs since she was five years older) so we're able to dance around to music. This was only one enjoyable flashback, I can remember. He was a fun, caring dad in public since he wouldn't get totally inebriated and show his true side.

Our dad's abuse came to a halt for the reason he never came home. My mom barely talked to him, as if they were living separate lives. Of course, this would happen, after I became mature enough to want to behave, listen and stay out of trouble.

Glimpse of Pure Love within Companions

At this moment, Dad was MIA the majority of their marriage and wasn't present to disagree in adopting animals. Colleen and I constantly begged Mom to adopt a domesticated animal. When she finally caved in, a cat appeared sitting at the front door. Since she was a stray (no collar or tags), we welcomed her inside, fed her milk and named her Taby. Taby was extra ordinary because she would always ring the doorbell to be let inside. That same year, one of the college students my mom knew found a dog in the mountains. Knowing she couldn't keep the puppy while attending college, so my mom offered to adopt her. We named her Ginger.

Instantly, I became attached to these wonderful creatures and the unconditional love they portrayed. Ginger followed me wherever I went, showed affection by licking my face, and was excited to see me getting off the bus with her tail wagging a mile a minute. Taby constantly purred and weaved in and out of my legs to be petted. I felt the connection with these beautiful animals but unfortunately, both animals did not survive beyond a year. The only upside to the downfall, we were able to keep one of Taby's offspring. Keeping the kitten filled the void from losing the most amazing animals we once had.

Moving Forward in Elementary School

I still had no interest in school; apparently, I daydreamed constantly or conversed too much. Even though I still received check minuses, I passed readiness first grade. This teacher had more patience than the previous one I had in kindergarten. I was also aware that I had to try my best to advance toward first grade because I didn't want to embarrass myself by repeating the same grade. My mom would not fight for me again, as she knows I had the ability to do better. Maybe I had ADHD, (back then doctors didn't diagnosis this in children) or this may perhaps, linked to the living conditions that caused my selective hearing and learning. Either way, I was putting in the effort to pass. It definitely wasn't because of friends I have made in the classroom; I can't recall one friend that I had made during the school year. Evidently, myself worth wanted to shine and push forward. And besides, I had friends in the neighborhood.

Summer time goes by way too fast, especially since I wasn't a scholar of a student. Every year during summer breaks, there wasn't anything exciting happening except for hot climate and playing with friends. Dad was and will always be considered a narcissist jerk, and controlled everything, so we never went on family vacations. He emphasized it's a waste of money.

Escaping the House of Horror with Vacation

The summer of 1975, my mom saved enough money selling Avon. She started becoming more confident and adamant with my dad's lack of empathy. He was never present thus the hell with him, she would say. At the age of seven, I experienced my first vacation. She shopped at a sporting goods store and bought a nice size tent, along with camping equipment like sleeping bags, portable grill, oil lamps, coolers, and floating rafts. After my sister and I (Doreen was only one at the time) helped organize our belongings in the vehicle, Mom drove to Wildwood, New Jersey, for the weekend. My aunt and her two boys joined us. The two sisters pitched their tents, and we devoured our lunch. After that, we hopped in Mom's vehicle and drove directly toward the beach. The weather was gorgeous, hot and sunny, perfect day to spend at the beach. My mom and aunt picked the ideal spot, located directly at the edge of the ocean. I laid my long beach towel down, lathered up with sunscreen and put on a life jacket. Colleen, our cousins and I grabbed a raft, and raced into the water. Forgetting the whole thing that Mom warned me not to do in salt water, as I did both, my eyes stung from opening them underwater and the taste of salt water was horrible! The entire day, I was mesmerized by the enormous waves! The twinkle in my eyes, verified this vacation was going to be the best time in my entire life! After becoming a prune from being in the water, I decided to dig in the sand. My mom and aunt brought plastic shovels plus sand castle buckets. I spent most of my afternoon filling the buckets up with water and sand to build the most amazing princess castle that would have caught your eye. Later in the day, my cousins had a field day burying me in the sand. I was the only brave one since Colleen was too scared. All you could see was my small head! I enjoyed hanging out with my cousins; they were a lot older, which always made me feel cool hanging out with them. In my eyes, this day was spectacular, but it was coming to an end. The sun was going down over the horizon and almost dinner time. We were planning on coming tomorrow, so I didn't squabble for departing. Although, we assumed we were, until mother nature took over.

After we arrived at the campsite, we heard on the news broadcast that there was a severe storm within the vicinity. My mom and aunt looked as if no worries, it shall move through quickly. We proceeded to cook dinner, get showers, and crawl into our sleeping bags since everyone was worn out from a great day. The storm rolled in overnight and the rain came barreling down. Over the course of hours of torrential downpours, our tent started floating like a raft in the ocean, along with our sleeping bags. My mom instructed us to get in the car and that's where we ended up sleeping. When we woke up the next day, the rain continued, so my mom and aunt decided to pack up our belongings. I was devastated and pouted all the way home. My mom reassured us we would go on vacation again, and we did. The following summer, we went back to Wildwood, New Jersey. My aunt and cousins joined us again too. There was never a dull moment when both families came together. Leaving their husbands behind, there was so much laughter, peace, and joy; this is why we vacationed together. Not to mention, the two sisters were inseparable.

My Mom's Perseverance

During the year 1976, for the second time, everything seemed to be eerily normal. Like a black cloud lifted over us. My dad still lived in between home and Tioga County. Mostly in Tioga, but still a narcissistic jerk even in his absence. He had control over all finances which he only allowed Mom to spend bare minimal amount on all necessities. Only at this point, Mom found the courage to withdraw from her abuser. She persevered without looking backwards, as if her inner being smacked her over the head and woke her up. Encouraging her to stop being the victim. The change happened instantly, as if her confidence and self-worth blossomed like a flower in the springtime. The day of her 30th birthday, she looked into the mirror and said, "Mirror, mirror, on the wall, are you going to put up with his bullshit anymore?"

She responded right back, "Hell, no!" When my dad came home the following weekend, he discussed moving the whole family to Tioga, so he wouldn't have to travel back and forth any more.

Mom's precise response, "Over my dead body!"

No questions asked, my dad said, "Then sell the house."

Struggles of Having Divorced Parents

Emotionally Challenged

While walking down a road, if any stranger glanced in my direction, they would automatically assume I was a normal, optimistic nine years old girl. But my inner child felt the total opposite.

I felt indifferent when my parent's divorce was final on May 26, 1977. During childhood, there was never consistency, nurturing, or peaceful time in my life. Now, I have another change I was required to get accustomed to. As I was getting older, I started blocking out recollections of all the childhood trauma I endured. The only thing I couldn't block out was my insecurities and loneliness within. Being outside and becoming an animal lover of all kinds, big or small, and saving wild little critters helped bring a little love and joy into my life. My mom sold the house, divided the funds between my dad and herself, and rented a half of a house in downtown Hershey, PA. Our residence was on one side of the house and the owner lived on the other side. Our new home wasn't far from where we previously lived, so I was able to attend the same elementary school. Even though, I didn't have friends in the classroom, I was still glad I didn't have to switch schools. Once again, our new neighborhood didn't have children my age to interact with, so I spent most of my free time outside walking around, muttering quietly. The only positive outcome of moving to this location was being able to walk to school, since it was only a mile down the road.

My dad moved to Tioga, since that's where the construction company he worked for was located. His girlfriend moved into his home, which my mom had suspected she was the one he had been unfaithful with during his travels.

The child custody agreement stated in the courts granted my mom full custody, but my dad had visitation rights every other weekend and public holidays. He decided not to carry out with what the courts stated in the contract; he became an absent father like he has always been both mentally and physically. My little sister's birthday was during the summer of their divorce and he never called or sent a birthday card. He could have died from alcohol poisoning, and we would have never known.

Did you ever buy one of those butterfly kits for your children, where you can actually watch the transformation of them being in a chrysalis state, evolving into a caterpillar, and then, the final stage, a beautiful butterfly? After twelve years of feeling trapped inside, scared, and afraid of life, my mom has finally become that butterfly. Her new-found freedom has just begun. But, did it really? Being a single parent, with three children, an absent father, the only freedom she truly had was from the abuse that she had endured that set her free.

I eventually became acclimated with my new surroundings. I still didn't have children my age to play with, therefore I spent most of the time wandering around the neighborhood. While doing so, I found my favorite place that wasn't far from home. It was a small piece of land that wasn't developed. It always felt peaceful as I lay there in the tall grass, daydreaming. Although, one afternoon, when I returned, before nestling in my favorite spot, I happened to look down and found a nest of baby chipmunks. I sat there quietly and looked around for their mom. She was nowhere in sight. I felt sad as they were abandoned and could die, so I ran home as fast as my little legs could take me. I rummaged throughout the house looking for a box so I could nurture them. I eventually found the perfect size, and when I returned, the mom was still absent, so I gently placed the nest inside. After arriving home, I showed my mom what I found and begged her to let me keep them until they were independent enough to be released into the wilderness. I had to beg and plead a million times before she finally agreed. I found a medicine dropper in the bathroom vanity and fed them warm milk periodically throughout the day. Eventually, they matured enough to survive on their own, so I released them into the wild. That was such a proud moment, I will never forget.

My mom was also getting acclimated with her new life and freedom as well. She landed a position at a food distributor as an office clerk, and discovering new-found friendships. Being single at thirty, and free, she started going out dancing and meeting men. Whenever, she would come down the stairs in her green, shiny polyester jump suit, and in a good mood, we knew she had a date. I didn't mind her going on dates, (although, I never slept until she came home) what I did mind and felt very uncomfortable, was when they spent the night. I had mixed emotions come to the surface that I couldn't control. I felt insecure, protective, and jealousy. I now had a new feeling, I disliked men. I would cry myself to sleep, wishing this feeling would go away. I never shared with her how I felt, since I was taught at a very young age not to show emotions or I would get punished.

As a single parent, working full time, going out on dates and socializing with friends; my older sister (Colleen is five years older) always babysat, portrayed in place of the mother role. She was pushed into this rollway too young, as she started at the age of nine when my parents were still married. Our dad was never home, and my mom going door to door selling Avon.

One of the fond memories I experienced when my sister babysat would have been a night during the popular Fuzzy Few Carnival (which they still have the same carnival, fifty years later). The town held the event on the baseball grounds, adjacent to the high school. It's wasn't a very large area. With a blink of an eye, you went around a perimeter. There may have been six rides, if that, but had plenty of games and food trucks. My eyes were on the prize, not the rides! I had plenty of change in my pockets, ready to win! After trying most of the games, my favorite turned out to be, throwing the ping-pong into the fishbowls. I'm pretty certain the carnival ran out of fish for a prize, as I came home with a small white mouse instead. My mom was not thrilled having a mouse in the house, but she allowed me to keep it. I went to the store, bought a small hamster cage and food. I took exceptionally good care of the little critter; he was my companion. As I adored my new rodent, it learned how to escape from his cage! I was baffled because the plastic cage was very secured. Panic arose to the surface, since we had a cat in the house, which disliked me and would kill the mouse. I always took precaution while walking around my own home, afraid the cat would jump out and bite me. I looked around the house for days and finally caught the rodent underneath the sofa. He was alive and well, so I placed it back in the small cage. The following week, the same thing happened, again! At this point, I became angry instead of upset. In my awareness, I knew this mouse couldn't open the plastic cage by itself; nonetheless, it had! I stomped down the stairs, growling like a dog, and looked entirely over the house. Not to mention dodging the cat once again, since I was extremely scared of him. I would scan each room before I proceeded in looking for Houdini of a mouse. This cat hated me for no apparent reason! He would corner me, with this angry look on his face and wag his tail, like I was his prey, ready to pounce! So, I didn't risk strolling near him, I always walked the opposite direction. The little mouse was MIA for a week until I found him underneath the refrigerator. The cat again, didn't do his job, thank God! After I found him, my mom talked me into doing what she believed was correct, letting him go outside into the wild. Explaining, he wanted outside the entire time, that's why he kept escaping. After contemplating and emotionally upset, I left my friend outside to run free, like I did with chipmunks. Come to find out later, my mom was the culprit the entire time!

It was that time again, and in my perspective, summer time zooms by to rapidly! Some children love heading back to school after vacation, I definitely despised it. I'd rather be outside, not cooped up inside a classroom. Also, deep down, I believed I was an outcast, because the girls wouldn't associate with me. I just started third grade, and only two months into school, my mom informed us we would be moving again. She purchased this newly constructed home trailer located in a decent size trailer court. The only downfall, it was located outside the school district we were in. We drove over to the trailer court numerous times in order to get us familiarized with our new community. The excitement Mom kept displaying never rubbed off on Colleen and I. Both of us experienced a sense of dismay regarding out transfer, because once again, we were leaving our familiar surroundings.

Being single and raising three young girls, Mom became

overjoyed with one of her biggest accomplishments; obtained her very own home. If she only knew beforehand, of what I was about to be subjective to; formerly making this decision and raising me in this kind of environment. I believe she would have had second thoughts. We moved into our new home Halloween weekend. The neighborhood was huge, compared to what I was accustomed to. This trailer court was spiral in shape and it felt similar to riding a sit-n-spin. You would go around and around until you were dizzy or when your equilibrium is off balanced. The outlines of all the existing homes acquired diverse colors, sizes, but mostly the same shapes; also, really close in proximity. It felt like you could reach out and touch one another. Our new neighborhood was in the middle of nowhere, all you could see were cornfields and a campground that ran along the property line which had a swimming pool. The style of our home, in my eyes, resembled a long comfortable hallway, horizontal and narrow. Not one peak, valley, upstairs, or downstairs. The color of the siding was yellow and white and was located on the outer edge of the trailer park. I loved the privacy with cornfields behind us, not neighbors. In the front of our home trailer had two paved parking spaces including a black lamppost with the house number pasted on it. With automobile parking limited, violators would be subject to tow. Our short sidewalk led to a small wooden deck with a flight of stairs to the front door. After you proceeded through the main entry, you would be standing in both rooms, the living room and kitchen. It was an open floor plan, with a breakfast nook that divided the two rooms. Mom's bedroom was right next to the kitchenette along with her own half bath. The other two bedrooms (which I had to share one with Doreen) and full bathroom was down the hall from the living room. Again, we were still living in the '70s so the colors of the walls and appliances weren't the best. Everything was yellow except the living room, which had dark brown paneling on the one side. I wasn't fond of that wall since it gave me a feeling of living in a dungeon; dark and dreary. Although, that style became popular in the late seventies. After we relocated, I became ecstatic in our new home and development. There were so many children, I felt like I was living in Disneyland! They were of all ages, from babies to young adults. Only then, it became my mission to find playmates. I was extremely grateful Mom gave me a new bicycle for my birthday. I truly required the means of transportation in order to get around this huge development and socialize. I only had the weekend to get acquainted with my surroundings and find children around my age, as I had to begin elementary school scheduled on Monday. My mission was accomplished, as new friendships started forming. Monday rolled around too quickly, and I had walk into a new third grade classroom that had remained in session for two months. I really didn't sleep that night as I was tossing and turning and my mind wouldn't rest. I was afraid of walking into a new classroom, children staring at me and having a new teacher, my poor stomach was in knots! I was already awake when my mom knocked on the door, and advised me to get out of bed. I was so nervous that I barely ate breakfast, as I was afraid the food would come right back up. I felt some relief when my mom advised me that she would be driving me to school and walking me to the classroom. Normally, I would ride a bus from the entrance of the trailer court, but I think she assumed it was best to assist me on the first day.

Shining Light

I walked into the classroom scared to death until the teacher, Miss Nicks, invited me into her new classroom. She was young, with short blonde hair, had this calming aura about her, and it seemed to take away all the butterflies that I had felt in my stomach. She then introduced me to the class and showed me to my seat. During the entire first day, I couldn't believe what I was feeling inside. I started on the road to enjoying school! The entire classroom sat together at lunch-time, and we had a twenty-minute recess to play on the playground. I had made friends rapidly (I'm still friends with some to this day)! This was one of the best days of my life, and I came home beaming, ready to explain the excitement to my mom.

I had been through hell and back as a child, but now, I was starting to spread my wings and fly. My loneliness was slowly dissipating, as I was finding some light within me to shine. Every now and then, even with some of that light within me, there was still a twinge of darkness that I battled thru periodically. I grew up way to fast, witnessing abuse, by abuse, and in addition facing situations no child should ever have to. Finally, feeling life as a normal kid was totally new to me and loved every minute of it! I was in all my glory with the new school and neighborhood, as I was making friends with both genders. My grades were improving, and I started coming out of my shell. Throughout the school year, the same group of girls and I would hang out during recess and lunch. Eventually, I was invited to my friend's home after school for a play date. I was thrilled, as I never had close friends like this before, or even a play date. I remember, taking her school bus home and the minute we strolled into her parent's house, I gasped. "Is this a mansion?" My friend started laughing as so did her father who had just made homemade chocolate chip cookies. Hot, just out of the oven, they melted inside my mouth. Their dining room was right next to the kitchen where I was eating the cookies and when I looked up, they had this beautiful crystal chandelier dangling from the ceiling. I had never seen anything that beautiful in my life! The sunlight was hitting the crystals just right; displaying different colors and shapes of the crystal balls and projecting them onto the wall. I was so mesmerized by the beauty; my friend had to yank me away to play. After my mom picked me up, I was still shocked over the size of their house compared to ours. One of my very first play dates, made the perfect way to finish the day.

 I wasn't the only one in the family that was feeling some sense of normalcy and excitement. My mom started a new job at the Capital Area Intermediate Unit. A unit for kids with special needs. Even though her position was a secretary, during her lunch break, she would make a point to go and interact with these children. Her mission every day was to make them smile, laugh, and just feel loved. Some of the children were warded of the state because they didn't have family. This one particular little boy, my mom grew incredibly fond of was named Bobbie. He didn't have parents, so she would bring him home for the day, even around holidays. We all adored and loved him, subsequently; he became part of our family. Unfortunately, he went into foster care, and Mom never communicated afterwards.

 My mom formed a friendship with a woman (still are to this day) whose home was located five trailers down from ours. She had three young boys; one my age and the other two were closer to Colleen's age. Both were single parents of three children and victims of spousal abuse. The two women met for a reason and became best friends as their survival to live and perseverance pushed them through the struggles of single parenting, as well as supporting one another became therapeutic.

Everyone in the family, including my sisters, seemed to be advancing forward and not looking back to what was. We opened up to this opportunity of living a new world. Unfortunately, with every light that shined through, came darkness because once again, I had to encounter heartache and disappointment.

Visitations with Dad

It had been a couple of years since we moved, and my dad was mostly absent through our young lives. I can only remember a hand full of times when he would engage with us kids. One day, he asked my mom's permission to visit, she agreed, and he appeared inebriated. My mom called the police to have him removed and that was the extent of our visit. For the most part, his visits consisted of him gracing us with his presence and then leaving. We were never invited to his residence, until mid-March when it was forced upon him during the 1979 Three Mile Island Nuclear evacuation. The area we lived was in the radius of evacuation, so we stayed at my aunt's house for a couple days. Then we had proceeded to my dad's home. He was not thrilled with this arrangement, since it was forced upon him, therefore drove us back home the very following day. Evacuation in the area was a week but we were home within three days.

Summer came, and Dad must have had a change of heart, because he invited us to visit for the weekend. I was so excited to finally spend quality time with him, but disliked where he resided. The town consisted of one gas station and one restaurant. The area was completely surrounded by mountains, with cabins nestled in the mountain-tops without running water or electricity, which were rented or owned by big game hunters. That's how deserted this town was.

He followed through on what he promised for a change and brought us to his home for the weekend. When we approached his double-wide trailer, his girlfriend and daughter came outside to greet us. They were all excited to see us again, since Dad made our visitation cut short the previous time. The first weekend we ever spent with him, and it turned out to be the weekend from hell! Our bonding time consisted of watching him get inebriated from sunrise to sunset; by then he was passed out for the evening. Luckily, there were children living next door that we played with in order to occupy our time. His girlfriend didn't drink (hallelujah), so one afternoon she decided to take us to seven-eleven for frozen ice (our excitement for the weekend). She asked our dad if he would mind, and his response was, absolutely not! He didn't want to waste his money on frozen ice. Ignoring his request, she took us anyway and paid with her own money. He was too inebriated when we arrived home, so he never noticed we were gone. The next afternoon, he decided to have a cook out, so we all jammed in one car and went to the grocery store. I believe, it was about a thirty-minute or more car ride until we finally arrived at the store. Whatever we needed for the picnic, he threw in the cart; hot dogs, hamburgers, potato salad, macaroni salad, buns, and all the condiments. It took us most of the afternoon until we returned home and started cooking. It was a nice midafternoon, even if it was just to the store and back. He was actually pleasurable for a change and joking around; a little glimpse of what he's like without all the alcohol he consumes. Dinner was ready, and frequently during a picnic, you sit together outside and enjoy family discussions. Definitely not there, they put us kids outside while they stayed indoors. We didn't even get to serve ourselves in what we actually wanted to eat; instead, Dad controlled what food we needed to consume. When he sat the plates down in front of us, immediately my little sister and I glanced at each other, making an *ewe* face to the potato salad; knowing we were in trouble because he would make us devour everything on the plate. Frozen in our seats, you could see the wheels turning in our heads, on how to get rid of this potato salad. He didn't have a dog to give it to or a trash can outside to throw it away. We were starving and dismissed the thoughts about this dilemma, so we ate around the potato salad. During dinner, both of us looked up at the same time and saw his girlfriend's daughter eating the potato salad. A light bulb went off in our heads, and both of us said at the same time, let's give it to her, she likes it; Dad will never know! Well, that was a big mistake, because Dad caught me in the act, when he came outside to check on us. Then he yanked me out of the chair so fast, my head was spinning. I kept yelling, "Please, Dad, don't hit me!" I tried so hard to wiggle my way out of his grip, but his strength kept me from fleeing. Obviously, he didn't listen, and proceeded to spank my butt with his bare hands, until I was black and blue. I showed no emotion, because if I did, he would give me something to cry about. After the discipline, I scurried toward the children next door and hid in their house until he passed out. He drove us home the very next day, and I advised my mom I never wanted to visit him again!

I believe children of age should have a voice in the court system, when it comes to which parent they choose to reside, and their visitation rights. If they had heard my voice, there would be no way in hell; my dad would have had visitation rights!

It was over New Year's Eve, the same year from the last visit, but this time, it was forced upon us girls, to spend the holiday with our dad. Neither of us felt comfortable around him, and we didn't want to spend any more length of time in his presence, then we had to. I preferred being home in a safe environment with my mom and friends; I'm a hundred percent certain, my sisters felt the same way. I must have blocked this trip from memory because the only thing I can remember was the night of New Year's Eve. Dad decided last minute, he wanted to spend New Year's Eve with his friends. He didn't trust us home alone, so he made arrangements for us to overnight at his buddy's house; they had children too. But when we arrived, they were older boys, more Colleen's age. Instantly, I felt uncomfortable. Later that evening, I couldn't hold back my emotions and started sobbing uncontrollably.

I asked the boys if I could use their phone, and they replied, "As long as it's not long distance." I dialed the operator, and she transferred the collect call to my mom. After she accepted the call, I was still sobbing hysterically; I could barely get the words out of my mouth but ended up shouting, "I need you to pick me up!" While explaining the situation with how Dad left us stranded with unfamiliar children and home; she proceeded to advise me that it would have been against the law to interfere with his visitation rights. I rung in 1980, with hopelessness and despair.

Generally, my childhood days, I have been consistently on an emotional journey with Dad. All a child wants is to feel loved and protected from their father, I received neither. Some days, there might have been a small glimmer of hope, but every time, I was disappointed. I identified that alcohol controlled his life and changed his temperament. He had a choice, alcohol or being a loving, devoted father; unfortunately, alcohol won. The New Year's Eve visit was the last incident for me, as I never wished to see him again. I also, couldn't ignore one of my horrific secrets I have been carrying within. I found the strength to persevere, and not be horrified that I would be dead, if I spoke to anyone regarding the sexual abuse.

I became very anxious and started shaking, as I advised my mom that I needed to tell her something. Just before the conversation began, tears streamed down my cheeks, I proceeded to tell her every detail of what occurred the night my dad engaged in sexual activity with me. During the discussion, if he had been standing in the same room, she would have murdered him with her bare hands. Her face turned bright red, the vein in the middle of her forehead stuck out, and shaking tremendously; it took all her strength not to drive to his house and murder him. Instead, she calmed down enough to pick up the telephone and call. Surprisingly, he answered the call, and she exploded! The pitch of her voice, I'm sure the whole town could have sensed the distress she was in. Of course, he denied the allegations and nothing was resolved, except we never had to visit him ever again. Even though he denied the encounter, I felt some relief yet sorrow at the same time. The relief, of not having weekend visitations with him, but sad because my dad would never be a part of my life.

The Trickle-Down Effect

Young Girl Struggles

From childhood to adolescence, I struggled inside, in a number of ways. Half of the time, I didn't know if I was coming or going. One part of myself sought to be a "born-again" child, wild and free; while the other felt grown-up, and not by choice. My emotions were like a knot of yarn at the pit of the stomach, trying to unravel one piece at a time, but tight enough where it wouldn't budge. Expressing emotions was nonexistent; as that's what I was taught at an awfully young age. Eventually, heartless actions appeared in my behavior.

After my mom learned about the sexual encounter from my dad, she thought it would be best for me to speak to a therapist. Periodically, the therapist invited my family to join in the discussion. I myself didn't think it had changed my outlook or conduct because I was hiding another secret.

This secret was something I never wanted my mom to find out, since the issue could damage the close-knit bond between the two sisters. My aunt had Multiple Sclerosis and was a severe alcoholic. She would start drinking the moment she awoke until she passed out in the middle of the night. My uncle was the exact same way. I didn't mind being around them while they consumed alcohol, as they were happy or sappy drunks, not terrifying like my dad. We would drive to their house for the weekend and assist with anything my aunt needed or ran errands; as her MS was getting life threatening. Their home was definitely the party house of the block because the entire neighborhood would come over to play cards and drink alcohol till all hours of the night. My two cousins, their friends, and Colleen would proceed down into the finished basement and play pool, while Doreen and I had to stay upstairs since my cousins stated, we were too young. The sleeping arrangements in their house was never an issue, since they had multiple bedrooms to divide everyone into. It started out wonderful having my own room, as if I was in heaven, since I had to share a bedroom with Doreen. Unfortunately, heaven turned out to be hell extremely fast!

These horrific incidences happened numerous times whenever Mom would tuck me into bed. It didn't matter which bedroom she placed me in; he would always locate where I was. Not soon after my mom would leave the room, my one cousin would slowly open the door and tiptoe over towards the bed. I froze and pretended I was sleeping the entire time, in fear of remembering what my dad had advised me. He then proceeded to remove my pajama bottoms and underwear in order to engage in sexual activity. After he finished, he pulled up my pajamas and exited the room without saying a word. During these encounters, I felt horrified and confused because, once again, I was stripped of my innocence by someone I trusted. The next day, he portrayed like nothing ever happened, and my lips were sealed.

Since I didn't want to be sexually abused anymore, I would make up excuses and refuse to visit their home. Instead, I would stay with friends while the rest of the family went to visit. The only sad part about my refusal was giving up quality time to spend with my aunt, as I knew, she wouldn't be here on earth that much longer. We had a close bond, and I enjoyed her company, even though she was an alcoholic. I wasn't able to consult with my therapist regarding my cousin, so I remained closed off to the world. My feelings had not changed; I disliked men, felt insecure, lonely, protective, and very sad even when the sessions were completed. I know first-hand that these sessions were not affective, just by the turmoil that occurred, from my mom's last date.

    I can recall, one Friday evening, Mom dressed nicely for her date. She threw out the green style polyester jump suit, as the style altered over the years. Now her new outfit was pink polyester pants with a pink floral blouse to match. She looked gorgeous all dressed up and make-up on. Whenever she dressed sexy, her disposition changed to enthusiasm. Colleen was scheduled for babysitting duty, which became a pleasant evening. The previous time she watched over us, Colleen decided to tie Doreen and I to our beds with rope and compelled us to swallow vinegar, because we didn't pay attention! To this day, I have no idea where she learned this punishment, but it was ineffective. Whenever Mom departs with her date, I know it's going to be a late night when she returns. After their date, I heard them come in the front door. They were tiptoeing and whispering as they were walking around the house so they wouldn't wake us up. I never grew out of the habit of waiting until she returned for the evening. I snuck out of bed, and walked over to her bedroom. The door was cracked enough for me to peak through and noticed them hugging and kissing. I instantly knew what happens next since I have witnessed it before; he was spending the night. Every one of these emotions that I tried to keep hidden, came toward the surface. I ran onto my top bunk, and started weeping. This time, I lost all control from all the bottled-up emotions that caused a full-blown temper tantrum. It felt like a forever tantrum, as I was mentally and tangibly exhausted; this feeling within me wouldn't dissipate. I personally couldn't believe Doreen didn't awaken from all the noise, since she slept on the lower bunk. Eventually, my mom was furious with my behavior, as she heard me from her bedroom. She came stomping down the hallway, swung the bedroom door open so hard, it put a hole in the wall. She then proceeded to yell at the top of her lungs regarding my behavior, slapped my face an adequate amount to split my lip open, and said, "Keep it up, and I'll give you more to cry about!" I was totally in shock when she hit me that hard, which caused a fat bloody lip; immediately, I stopped crying and just laid there emotionless. I finally fell asleep, feeling sad and lonely.

The Infamous Trailer Court

Living in a trailer court and socializing with friends I made, was very different from the ones I had in elementary school. It felt as though I was leading a double life. Most of the children within the trailer court also came from dysfunctional families, just like mine. Most of them were older, by at least four years. The ones I had met, we had lot in common; maturing too fast, abuse and getting into mischief. Some of the children also had single parents, which allowed them more freedom due to their employment, in order to support the families. Then, my elementary school friends; I would visit their family home, they had parents with more structure and discipline. Those friends seemed to come from a normal, loving, and stable environment; their innocence wasn't taken away from them, (not that I know of anyway) like mine. They were living the childhood dream, exactly what I would love to have. This was how my child's eye perceived and felt inside regarding the two groups of friends. My behavior in each environment showed proof I was leading a double life and sometimes became a bad influence on the innocent. If I was inside my home, it wasn't by choice, as I absolutely loved being outdoors, whether it was summer or winter. If my mom couldn't find me outside play-acting in the yard, all she had to do was look up, and find me in a tree. Wilderness was in my blood, and so was curiosity. Curiosity got me every time but not always in a good way.

One fall day, I was around ten years old when there was a group of us walking around the campground; it was adjacent to our neighborhood, and for some reason the campground was the place to hang out. As we were walking around, laughing, having a good time; one of the girls pulled out a marijuana joint. I stood there and watched while they passed it around. When it came my turn, I contemplated for maybe a second or two and then I took the joint. I never smoked in my youthful days, (my mom smoked cigarettes) and had no idea how to inhale, I tried it anyway. Well, I must have inhaled wrong or it just gagged me, but I started coughing hard enough where I almost threw up in my mouth. They all burst out laughing like hyenas, which didn't facilitate the situation. Everyone was stoned but myself, since they seemed to be experts in smoking pot. Later, they developed this brilliant idea and wanted to climb on the campground store's roof. I didn't have to be stoned to enjoy this, as I loved climbing on things. The store was closed at that moment; therefore, we all climbed to the peak of the roof. We stayed up there for quite some time, conversing with one another. There was no damage to the store, but somebody must have snitched on us, because a week later, my mom received an eviction notice in the mail. After she addressed this matter (there was no damage), the owner of the trailer court decided to schedule a probation period instead. I ended up being grounded for a couple weeks.

Another time, I can recall, the same group of friends built a small fort made out of sticks and mud in a no trespassing zone. It was the only secluded area we could find to give us privacy. You had to crawl under the fence, go through some thistles in order to get to the other side which belonged to the farmers. It was close to my home but far enough, where my mom couldn't see us going in and out. The location was perfect as it was in a small wooded area, right before you come to the open cornfields. The trees must have blocked it enough, because the farmers never noticed it and neither did my neighbors. This fort, turned out to be one of our best secret hideout places ever made; we drank alcohol, smoked pot, and looked at porn magazines. Hanging with an older more "mature crowd," sometimes came with consequences too. I will never forget this one incident that scared me half to death. I was walking with a group of boys and girls through the campground and the boys started expressing interest on the subject matter regarding puberty, asking us girls how much pubic hair we had.

I didn't engage in the conversation, but one of the boys, who was in high school and looked like a giant compared to myself, looked straight at me and verbalized, "I bet you developed a bushel of pubic hair!" When I didn't answer back, he pulled me down to the ground laughing and kept repeating, "Let me see, let me see!" I was trying to fight him off, telling him no, but he was too over powering.

Ultimately, he was able to pull down my pants, gazed, made the comment, "Yep, I was right," and walked away. I was in complete shock and disbelief of what just transpired. Everyone just stood there without assisting me with my attacker. After I pulled up my pants and didn't engage with anyone, I headed home. I felt ashamed, blamed myself, for hanging out with such a crowd, but I still continued to and never told anyone in my family what happened.

My inner child wanted to come out and play, and have some kind of normalcy, which it only happened, when I went to school. I became very close with a small knit group of girls from elementary school. We all decided to join brownies, which gathered together once a week after school hours. There was a book of all kinds of badges we had to produce and sometimes we would venture out on day trips. Once we had enough badges on our sash, we were promoted to Girl Scouts. I was so excited to be a Girl Scout as I loved camping and being outdoors. This was where I belonged; friends, camping, cooking outdoors, and hiking. Parents were able to join us to be counselors; I was excited to have my mom be one of them.

One time, my mom was a counselor during our camping trip, and located at the campsite were two types of sleeping arrangements you were able to choose from. One was a huge cabin with an enormous grey stone fireplace, bunk beds that were lined up on both sides of the cabin, complete bathroom and kitchen. The other building was and open-air rustic A-frame with only hardwood floors to sleep on. I wanted to attempt something new, so I talked my girlfriends and my mom to sleep outside in the A-Frame as it was a warm beautiful summer night. They all agreed, so we snuggled into our sleeping bags for the night. My mom was the first one to fall asleep, but us children were occupied by chit chatting and laughing as usual. One of the girls mentioned out of the blue, "What if a stranger comes out of the woods to grab us?"

They all shrieked and got scared. Trying to calm everyone down, I said, "Let's make a booby trap with the broom over there; she'll wake up if it falls." So, we set up our booby trap and everyone started to feel at ease until one of the girls bumped it by accident, the broom fell to the ground, made a loud enough noise where it echoed through the woods. My mom never flinched at the noise as she was still snoring away. All the girls packed up their camping gear, ran as fast as they could to the cabin, and that's where they resided for the evening. My mom and I slept side by side, as I wasn't scared and didn't want to leave her behind.

A lot of my special memories came from being in Girl Scouts since we did everything that I loved to do, and it brought out the inner child in me, that has been hidden for so long. It kept me out of trouble, as we weren't smoking pot, drinking, or looking at porn magazines. Although, I personally recall getting into trouble one time, and it had zero to do with drugs or drinking. When we were camping, the counselors divided us up into different groups for a scavenger hunt. They gave us a list of all nature items that we needed to find, mark them off the paper, and bring them back. I was thrilled to be put in a cluster of my closest friends as we all got along. The instructions that were given to us before we ran off was, "Do not go past this certain point in the forest for safety reasons of getting lost."

When they said, "Move out." We bolted right into the forest, like we're looking for real treasure or gold. As we came upon the "do not pass" point in the forest, we all looked and read each other's minds, and walked right past the point of no return. The path we followed, luckily made a large loop, and we ended up back to the beginning of the trail. The only problem was it took us practically two hours until we arrived back at the cabin with nothing to share from the scavenger hunt list. The counselors appeared extremely upset when we arrived, which quickly turned into anger, considering we were all safe. They took us aside one by one, scolded, and separated us for the rest of the camping trip.

Getting into trouble, definitely wasn't my first rodeo (this incident was nothing compared to what I'm used to), as it might have been for the friends of mine. I was so thankful and relieved that after being separated for the weekend, we stayed friends, even after the anguish they may have encountered.

Subsequently, being in Girl Scouts for a couple of years and seeing how good it was for my soul, not to mention that it kept me out of trouble; Mom decided to send me to Girl Scout camp for a week (after I pleaded). Even though my mom struggled financially and worked multiple jobs, she gathered enough funds to pay the tuition. There were several weeks throughout the summer you could choose, and each week had different activities; such as horseback riding, swimming, hiking etc. I was lucky enough to get the calendar week I requested, and arrived as a happy camper. I did this for a couple of summers, and each year, I absolutely enjoyed the camp and made new friends.

Best Friend Forming

Out of the group of children I socialized with in the fourth grade, I became best friends with a cute little blonde-haired girl (also an identical twin), whom invited me over for my first play date (we're still friends to this day). Her name was Michelina. We instantly bonded, which was a remarkable feeling, as I never had a best friend before. We spent virtually every weekend together during summer time. She had this innocence and poise about her that made me laugh; she would follow along with whatever I did or say (which wasn't always the best thing). Whenever I would visit or sleepover at her house, we would do normal youth activities such as: play games, watch movies, go outside in her play area, trimming her bangs (her dad was not happy with how short they turned out), play dress up and dance around to music. My inner child was finally able to come out and play. Visiting her home, the insecurities felt nonexistent; the loneliness dissipated, and her parents loved me like I was their own. Acknowledging and feeling the difference between two separate spheres, I for one never wanted to go home. Most of the time, I would ask her if we could play at her house instead, and she agreed. But I do recall multiple times, I invited her to my house for sleepovers and that's when her innocence changed drastically. I didn't think we would stay friends afterwards; but we did.

Bad Influencer

The first time Michelina came to my home for a sleepover was normal; I showed her around the trailer court and introduced her to my friends. We kept busy riding bikes, walking or else skipping our way around the neighborhood, until both of us got hungry. We sauntered back to the house to make some lunch. I was so embarrassed because our cupboards were completely bare except for a container of oatmeal to cook. It was the complete opposite at her house since she had such a variety of food stacked to the hilt in their cupboards, and we literally had nothing in ours. Mom must not have received her paycheck yet, because that's the only time, we had food in the house. I asked her if she liked oatmeal, and said sure! Well, apparently, I had no clue what I was doing and horrible at following directions because I measured the salt wrong. When we took a bite, that's all we tasted, so we immediately spit it out into the kitchen sink. We laughed so hard that I thought we were going to pee in our pants. Since the oatmeal was absolutely disgusting, we decided to make peanut butter and jelly sandwiches instead. This was the one and only childlike day, she experienced at my home.

Our weekend sleepovers became a ritual until one day; we thought it was going to be shattered due to my mom's new employment. In July 1979, Hershey foods employed Mom, which was a great opportunity because her pay increased. Eventually, she would be able to pay off her debt and buy groceries without government assistance. The only downfall with her new employment was that on the low totem pole, she had to work the graveyard shift, eleven p.m. to seven a.m., Monday thru Friday. Overtime was voluntary but sometimes mandatory.

This shift was not ideal for eleven years old. Even though Colleen turned sixteen and had her license, summer came to a halt. My mom slept during the day, and Colleen worked, so I had no means of transportation. The playtime and sleepovers with Michelina came to an end, until one day I had a brilliant idea. For the reason that we were young, her parents wouldn't let her come over unless there was adult supervision. I instructed Michelina if she wanted to sleep over, we could keep it secret from her parents that my mom worked night. She went along without hesitation, regarding the concept and that's when she saw first-hand my other world. It was one of those hot and steamy summer days, when our plan became successful, and we're able to have a sleepover. It was scorching hot so the only thing we could accomplish outside was swimming at the pool, so that's where we headed. As we walked toward the direction of the campground pool, we were bypassing the fort that my friends and I built. I shouted, "Follow me, I want to show you something!" We went under the fence and through the thistles until we came upon the fort. She was amazed at the fort but when she saw the porn magazines, I thought her eyes were going to pop out of their sockets. Well, curiosity got her too, so we both sat there and paged through the magazines.

We laughed, and made comments like, "Hope our boobs turn out to be that big!" After we finished gazing at the magazines, we headed to the swimming pool. Most of the afternoon in the pool, the day consisted of playing Marco Polo or just hanging on the side talking about the magazines we rummaged through. There were a couple of neighborhood friends that appeared, and engaged in our conversation, as they already knew about the fort and magazines. After getting burnt to a crisp from the sun and looking like prunes, we decided to walk home and change out of our wet swimsuits.

During our departure, one of my friends yelled out, "Meet me later as soon as you get changed." Once we changed out of our wet bathing suits and grabbed a snack, we headed to my girlfriend's house. This friend of mine, was four years older, smoked pot, cigarettes, and drank alcohol. I did all the above, but I myself never smoked cigarettes. We knocked on the front door, and she came outside complaining about an empty box of cigarettes. Having no indication how she purchased drugs or alcohol and not really caring, I suggested that we head back to my house, because my mom smoked, and I may possibly be able to take some cigarettes out of her box. She thanked me, and we walked back to my house. I made them stay outside, as my mom was still sleeping from working nightshift. I slowly opened the door as quietly as I could and tiptoed around the house looking for her box of cigarettes. I went through her jacket, the cupboards and all the rooms where she usually stashed them. I couldn't find them anywhere. She must have them in her bedroom. With no success, I came up with a different idea. I'll take out the cigarette butts that are in her ashtray; she never smoked them down to the end. I went outside with a handful of cigarette butts and my friend replied, "That will do!"

She turned around and asked Michelina and I if we wanted to try smoking and in chorus, we both said, "Sure!" We walked behind the house so we wouldn't get caught, and we didn't want to wake up my mom with our giggles. Since this was Michelina's first-time inhaling, immediately she coughed like I did, when I first smoked marijuana, but then she got the hang of it. Neither of us were thrilled with the taste of cigarettes; in fact, it left a nasty taste that lingered in our mouths forever. We both agreed we'd never try that again. After everyone was finished smoking, we tossed the cigarettes across the fence into the cornfield so my mom wouldn't find them. I never smoked cigarettes again and neither did Michelina.

I was very surprised after the first sleepover that Michelina would want to return to my home, but she did, and I was thrilled!

Once again, Michelina slept over, but this time, it was going to be different; there would be a couple of boys spending the night as well. It was a Friday night and my mom decided to order pizza. It was always a special treat when she did, since she struggled financially. I can recollect eating pancakes for dinner because she couldn't afford meats, but we managed to survive without the specialties. My mom had to work Friday nights, so she wanted to make sure we were fed and settled in before she left for work. This evening, was also the night, when we watched her co-worker's son because she worked nights too, and didn't want him alone all evening. Since he was going to be the only boy in the house, Mom allowed his friend to spend the night as well. She had trusted both boys since she was friends with their parents.

My mom left around ten p.m., and the boys showed up around the similar timeframe. The boys started out hanging out in my mom's bedroom watching TV, while us girls sat comfortably in beanbag chairs listening to music, calling the radio stations and requesting our favorite songs. It was getting late, so I instructed Doreen it was bedtime, so we could partake in some alone time. I don't recall where Colleen was that evening or if she ever came home. I convinced the boys to come out and join us. I knew both boys, but Michelina didn't, so she was shy at first. As the night proceeded, we all started getting comfortable with one another on an entirely different level; we started talking that resulted in sexual positions and private body parts. Eventually, we finished playing truth or dare. The first round of dares we made hoax phone calls. The second round became sensual; we had to kiss one of the boys and vice versa. The final round turned out risqué; we had to exhibit our personal bodily parts. After that the game ended, none of us seemed embarrassed about what transpired; in fact, we were so intrigued by the boy's penises that we asked them if we could feel it. What schoolboy would say no to that? So, they allowed us, and we were shocked at the way it felt; soft, squishy, and limp. We then proceeded to ask questions on how it percolates. The rest of the evening, that's all we talked about until we fell asleep. The next day, we were stunned from what transpired, but all of us kept it a secret, and it never happened again.

After seeing another world that I lived in and being a bad influencer, my best friend's feelings never changed; we were inseparable.

A Weekend with a Schmuck

Throughout the years, my mom was trying to find the perfect man. I personally believe she was looking around all the wrong places, or her self-esteem was still low. After the divorce from my dad, all the men she dated were schmucks. The one man she dated briefly went on a mini weekend get-away with our family. We stopped at a motel for the night, and he told Doreen and I, to go swimming. (Colleen stayed home to work) When we walked down towards the outdoor swimming pool, I noticed it was completely green with insects floating around everywhere. There was no way I wanted to plunge into that water. When I walked back to our room the door was locked. I pounded by the way of my petite fists, calling Mom, but no response. I walked back to the pool and told Doreen we were locked out of the room. My sister and I felt abandoned; therefore, we hung out on the patio, looking at the green water with insects floating in it. Subsequently after sitting on the broken lounge chairs being bored, steam started coming out of my ears because now, I'm livid. We mutually decided to walk back to the room and beat on the door again. When he finally unlocked the door, his hair was dripping wet, partially dressed and Mom was coming out of the bathroom putting a robe on. I wasn't naïve and knew immediately what they were doing while showering. Leaving us children alone outside in a strange area to have a quick rendezvous, I gave them both the evil eye and didn't engage in conversation the rest of the weekend. None of these men were up to my standards, except for maybe one and that didn't last very long.

Childhood Boyfriend

As my mom wasn't having any luck with men, or choosing the wrong type, I myself found my first boyfriend at the age of twelve. His name was Jim.

A cluster of us from the trailer court found a new place to go every Friday night; the roller-skating rink. Even though, they played organ music instead of rock-n-roll and had strict rules because an employee would blow the whistle if you're going to fast; we still enjoyed ourselves anyway. I believe it was freedom from our parents and something different to do, other than hanging around the trailer court, that drew us to the skating rink, The families would take turns carpooling, since it was a half hour away. Some of the parents would drop us off at the arcade, which was right down the street. We would play games and then walk down to the roller rink when it opened.

    This one particular Friday night as I was lacing up my roller skates, I stopped and glanced up to detect an unexpected guy staring at me. Straight away, I thought he was cute with his blonde curls and blue colored eyes. Therefore, I stared right back at him. Even though we made eye contact, in my mind, he wouldn't be interested in me since he perceived to be older than I was. I brushed off the encounter and went off to skate with my friends. The arena wasn't enormous; by the blink of an eye, you're already around one lap. It almost made you dizzy skating around and around a short loop. As the night progressed, I myself kept proceeding to cross paths among this stranger, but both of us were too busy with our friends and didn't engage. In time, I spotted him having a conversation with teenagers from my neighborhood. The entire night I was intrigued regarding the connection, because I knew he didn't go to our school, as I have never seen him before. I skated a couple more laps before I headed over to the concession stand to grab something to eat. There was a long line of customers, and while I was waiting, my neighbor skated right up behind. I personally couldn't hold back the curiosity, so I asked her, "Who's that young guy you're hanging out with, because he's cute."

Her response, "One of my cousins, do you want to meet him?" Then all of a sudden, I became nervous and shyness arose which never developed before. The word "yes" wouldn't come out of my mouth, so she skated off. At the end of the evening, I took off my skates and headed outside for my ride. As I strolled down the long wooden planks to get to the parking lot, there he was, waiting for his ride too. We stood there in awkwardness; the ice broke, when he started a conversation. Then his parents arrived just as we were getting comfortable. When he opened the car door, he turned around and asked me if I would be available the following day. If so, he would come over to his cousin's house, and we could get together. Just like I suspected, he was three years older than I was, but that didn't seem to bother him. The next day he was visiting his cousin's house, and we met in the middle of the trailer court where the playground stood. We must have been there for hours talking, because all of a sudden, the sun was setting. The curfew rule in our household was to be home before dusk. I did not realize how the time flew by, as it was getting dark. I literally jumped in mid-air off the swing and told him I needed to head home. He grabbed me, right before I started to run off, and kissed me. The curfew went right out the window as we stood there kissing until the sky went dark. I scurried home thinking the kiss was worth the consequences; I was grounded for a week. Unfortunately, the relationship didn't last very long as I crushed his heart. I pulled away, because of past feelings that emanated to the surface. The insecurity and trust issues with men, never disappeared, like I hoped. I know this was the case, because of the emotions I felt when he started dating someone else. There was sadness within and the feelings never dissipated.

Cursing Me with Church

It had been four years living in this neighborhood; and Mom was still trying to change my behavior. At one point, she thought going to church would help with my defiance. So, every Sunday there would be a bus that came through the neighborhood, picked up the children and take us to Sunday school. Once we arrived, everyone would walk into their classrooms. But with me, I walked right back out after asking the teachers if I could use the restrooms. I never returned until the end of session. The church was enormous with several places to hide and the classrooms were over capacity with children that the teachers never found or noticed I was gone. Obviously, her plan never worked, and she never found out about my little secret.

Moving into Solitude

By the summer of 1981, Mom had paid off her debt, and decided to move us into a better environment. She bought land, and moved our home trailer into a small village called Upper Lawn. It was in the middle of nowhere; all you could see and smell were farms. The neighborhood consisted of a row of homes, and most of the people were extremely religious that wore bonnets on their head and long dresses. I was in disbelief that she would have gone this far to keep me out of trouble. Not to mention, my grandparents would be moving next door. As I was becoming a teenager, my grandfather didn't scare me any longer; I just didn't feel comfortable visiting for any length of time. This was my new beginning? I felt like I was thrown in jail! I'm surrounded by religion with no friends, a new school, and living in Timbuktu.

New Beginnings

A Teen Growing Up

On the new property, my mom and grandparents had basements built, the exact same length of each trailer. The home trailers have wheels underneath, so she hired a tractor-trailer company to transport them, as well as a crane company to place them above the basements. The land she purchased was a half-acre lot that contained a steep hill located between the adjacent trailers. At the bottom of the steep hill, were beautiful full-grown Weeping Willow trees. The rest of the land consisted of pine trees and swampy areas when it rained.

Once again, my youthful life was disrupted, and I could only think of two positive outlooks of relocating; it was during the summer and not in the middle of my sixth-grade year.

After moving and getting situated, it appeared to be usual. The friends I had, previously, came to visit or spent the night, and the two little boys I babysat, their mother brought them to our new location. The days came and went, and before you knew it, school began again. All summer long, I was prolonging this reality and refused to come acquainted among my new surroundings. But here we are again, forced out of my comfort zone with a brand-new school and seeing strange faces.

The first day of sixth grade came too quickly! Fortunately, with the six grade every elementary school in the district intermixed their students within the middle school building. All the students were seeing new children, not only myself.

 Mom took me shopping the day before school began even though she despised the anguish I had always put her through. I dragged her into every clothing store looking for the perfect outfit. When I finally found one, I gazed down at the price; took a big gulp and felt my eyes bulge out of their socket. I couldn't resist, because this outfit was exactly what I was searching for. I gathered every dollar and cents that I made over the summer and purchase the outfit. I didn't sleep well that night, as I was nervous and excited at the same time. Nervous, not because of the new faces but because it was a huge school, and for the first time, we had to switch classes for different subjects. The only excitement I felt, was being able to wear my new outfit.

 On the first day, I walked down to the bus stop; and already, two boys were standing there waiting. It was completely silent when I approached and no one made eye contact. Talking about relief when the bus appeared, as it was completely awkward amongst us. As I strolled onto the bus, I found myself relieved to find an empty seat, or I would have to request a stranger to share theirs. The bus route had multiple stops since I lived in Timbuktu. I could understand how kids would fall asleep and miss their stop because it took me over forty minutes to get to school. When the bus pulled up to the middle school, my stomach sank to my feet and head started spinning. I'm going to get lost, which will make me late for class, was all I kept thinking. I received the class schedule by mail in August, which advised which team and class information I was assigned to. Feeling a little overwhelmed, I barely had the courage to depart the bus, and walk into this enormous building. Eventually as I'm taking deep breaths, marching around the halls, I found my homeroom. Instantly, when I sat down at the desk, girls started talking to me. I thought to myself, this transition isn't dreadful after all. Throughout the day, switching classes, each teacher affirmed their students to double-check their list of students to make sure everyone was present. They also advised us if we were running late the first week, we wouldn't be considered tardy. They understood, as we were getting acclimated with the new school and altering classes. The day surpassed my expectations because being late was one of my worst nightmares. When lunchtime arrived, I thought I died and went to heaven with the variety of food choices plus ice cream! I was undecided for most of the lunch period with the choices or what I could afford. By the time I sat down and devoured the meal, the bell rang, and the classes resumed for the day. I thought the hours of the day went by rapidly, enjoyed switching classes, and had diverse teachers. Not being a scholar most of my childhood, this could change.

Living in Timbuktu

During first year of living in solitude, which still felt like prison, I compelled to become more acquainted with my grandparents at a much profound level. Living beside them, we helped each other and it blossomed into a beautiful relationship. It took a while, but I was able to bring to the surface the tiny "child" that was buried deep within their souls. My grandfather, reminded me of "The Grinch That Stole Christmas," where his heart just grew and grew all through the numerous times of interacting with us. His toughness never subsided, but then again, recognized how to get to his heart. We invited him over to play card games. One of our favorites, and now his, was playing UNO. My sisters and I never seen him smile, much less giggle before, until we introduced him to this game.

My grandmother, had this sweet, loving and charismatic personality; but don't piss her off, because she liked to hold grudges. She demonstrated all her talents by crocheting beautiful Afghan blankets, knitted sweaters with matching hats and contributed some to the church. Her talents amazed me; so, one day, I enquired if she would teach me how to crochet an Afghan blanket. After rummaging through some outdated yarn, she taught me how to crochet. The colors that she gave me were horrid and didn't complement one another.

Nevertheless, it was the thought that counted and her time. After finishing the Afghan, I realized, creativeness was in the genes. Her personality was also entertaining since she played card games as well. In fact, she taught us how to play Pinochle. It wasn't one of my favorite games, but enjoyed the time we spent together.

Getting to know both grandparents, put a different perspective on how love is shown different ways, and how it trickles down through each family member. I was able to see past the tough love from my grandfather as we bonded; which resulted in some fun times! One day, he saw me unhappy because out of us three girls, Mom would always choose me to push mow the half acre yard. When I glanced up, I noticed him scampering out of his basement with his lawn mower, and started racing me. I realized at that moment, it's the little things in life that shows love. My mom is exactly like her father; she inherited his tough love, but now that I was getting older, I understood and accepted the love that was given.

The first year of middle school, I became adjusted pretty quickly; the teachers were astounding and the girls were sociable. I didn't have one best friend so far, but then again didn't let it discourage me. My grades were average hence the teacher's comments on the report card, (talkative and daydreamed excessively). My attitude regarding grades consisted minimum effort, so I didn't fall below average. Any student with below average to failing grades will not be able to attend the end of the year class field trip. The teachers informed their students from the beginning of the school year that we'll be going to Camp Hebron for a week in April. I would never let this incentive pass me by because of my grades; camping was in my blood (Not to mention, how embarrassing it would have been).

April came sooner than I expected, and I started packing my suitcase. Finally, the week arrived and turned out to be a gloomy rainy Monday morning. All the students, teachers and camp counselors, (which were high schoolers) gathered in the atrium with their camping gear, waiting for the bus transportation. The only disruption, within this week, was getting my wisdom teeth out; I needed to depart a day early. Not knowledgeable with camp expectations, I didn't realize a day would make a difference. Afterwards, when we arrived at the camp, the teachers divided both genders with individual councilors and proceeded to the cabins. There were at least ten kids assigned to one cabin. As my group proceeded forward, there stood bunk beds lined up against the wall; I felt like a tiny fish in a sardine can. The cabins were small and we all had to share a bathroom. Needless to say, I didn't shower often, but I didn't care, as I was acquired to get muddy anyway. The majority of the outside activities that were assigned, I had been familiarized with through girl scout camp, but enjoying the new adventures with classmates. As I was maturing, so was my competitive side and preferred activities like scavenger hunts. On a daily basis, each group was handed a list of items that were located in the wilderness. By the end of the week, the group that presented the most items won a prize. I was determined to win! Since I was a tomboy, my favorite mission the teachers instructed us to accomplish was wading through the streams with our fishnets in order to catch fish, frogs, snails, or any other marine life we could find. I overheard a lot of complaints with the girls, regarding this task, but I enjoyed wading in a filthy stream and catching marine life. Every meal, we gathered at the dining hall as the boys were strolling out. Boys were entirely separated from us during the duration, until the very last night, which I had to miss because of my wisdom teeth. Thursday morning when Mom arrived, all my friends kept emphasizing, how I'm missing the greatest evening of the whole week; a huge bon-fire, music, and finding a boy to make-out with. I was totally distraught when I departed the camp, but blissful that friendships were forming.

Getting wisdom teeth removed during such a young age, put a hindrance during my first year of middle school. The situation effected the last night at Camp Hebron and cheerleading try-outs. I already signed up and practiced cheers along with other students; but now I must address this matter with the head cheerleading coach. The doctor insisted during recovery, I needed to rest, and he declined cheerleading for a couple of weeks. I advised the coach of doctor's orders, and she walked away in disbelief. The following year at try-outs and the exact coach's demeanor frowned on me, given that, I wasn't chosen for the cheering squad. I refused to attempt the squad again, and instead I went out for Track.

With Track and Field, they exhibit numerous events, that I became overwhelmed. I never participated in any type of sport before, so I had no inclination of what my talents might be. During the first practice, I scanned all the events, and decided to join the long, triple, and high jumpers. After getting accustomed with all three jumps, I started enjoying all three events and the team. I definitely wasn't the best in fact, I was terrible since I never placed, but I still adored the entire team effort and support. Joining this amazing group was the best decision I have ever made; by doing so, best friends formed, and I found my first boyfriend during middle school.

Having a boyfriend in middle school is precisely comparable to changing your underwear, you have a different one every single day. Although, mine lasted maybe a week or so, and consisted of writing notes to one another during classes. The exchange of notes would be at our school lockers or passing each other in the hallway. I was accustomed to more than just notes in elementary school at the old neighborhood; but I followed through with the new ways of life. Apparently, break-ups were also written in note form; since I received mine and had been delivered by his best friend. My feelings were hurt because there wasn't any rhyme or reason, so I guess he just needed new underwear. It didn't take long to shift forward from the hurt or expectation, so the next day, the feelings subsided.

Everyone, in middle school, going through puberty; was seeking to engage in one another.

One of my best friends, Karina, would host house parties; her parents were frequently present, but never proceeded downstairs to examine the gathering, since they trusted Karina's judgement. As you gazed around both living rooms, there were conjoined bodies making out everywhere. It reminded me of shopping in the lunch meat aisle; pick a number when your turns next, since every party she hosted, each couple switched. I recall one party, taking along the assistant jumping coach as my date. I am certain that it would have been illegal, because he already graduated from high school. Our bodies were cuddled up on the leather recliner talking, but then he leaned forward for a kiss. Immediately after kissing, the attraction was gone. I was confused whether it had anything to do with his kissing or prickly mustache, but I sent him home with no regrets.

Hershey Park has been a great amusement park for over one hundred and fifteen years. This is where we would go and connect with others during the course of summer months. Unfortunately, Mom slept during the day and we had lived in Timbuktu, I would have to ride my bicycle into town in order to car pool with Karina. It felt like a never ending five miles going up and down hills, smelling cow manure from the farms, and sweating my little butt off. We would arrive as soon as the park opened and remained there until they closed. For each day, after being dropped off, our mission needed to be accomplished or we would end the evening in frustration. Our mission was connecting with a pair of boys, which had to be one blonde haired and the other dark brown. I always preferred the dark brown. Majority of the time our types corresponded. After introducing ourselves to the boys and the awkwardness, we all strolled throughout the park riding our favorite rides. Partnering up with strange boys apparently isn't a wise decision, as they're looking for more than a thrilling roller coaster ride, as I experienced it firsthand. One afternoon, we met some boys and rode the Coal Cracker. It's a floating water log, which seats around four people. We coupled up with our boys, and during the ride, mine decided to slither his hands under my shirt, touching my breasts! Immediately, shock ran through my body; I froze and became speechless, which is very rare for me. After the ride was finished, I yanked Karina toward one of the restrooms to explain what transpired, so we remained inside the bathroom exceptionally long, thinking the boys would depart and go their separate ways. We alternated with peeping out the restroom door to make sure the coast was clear, and then sprinted out as fast as our athletic legs could take us. Sprinting and laughing like hyenas shouldn't be combined, as I lost my breath and fell to the ground. Later that night, we ran into them at the arcade. I had nothing to say and completely avoided him, but the blonde asked Karina, why did we sprint out of the bathroom? Apparently, the coast wasn't clear, which made us chuckle the rest of the night, by our thought process and looking ridiculous trying to elude them.

Going to Hershey Park during the summer, you become acquainted with the employees, which some were high school students. I had my eye on one particular guy, who worked the pretzel stand. He wasn't my typical type with dark hair, as his was mousy brown, but I was enticed. Possibly, it may have been the blue polyester uniform that caught my eye, but it didn't matter at the time, since I was hormonal. After walking past his pretzel stand a million times, I developed enough courage to walk over and order a pretzel. We flirted back and forth as I received the change and pretzel but he didn't continue the conversation. Right before departing the stand, I asked if he was working until closing, and he replied, "Yes." Toward the end of the evening, I walked back to the pretzel stand and he was packing up, so I started a conversation. Right before leaving the stand, he asked me out on a date. It was a warm Saturday afternoon, when the pretzel guy pulled up in the driveway with his parent's conversion van. I took one glance at the van, and thought to myself, there is no way in hell I'm having sexual relations on my actual first date. I leaped in the van, looked over my shoulder, and noticed a couch bed in the back. My eyes rolled behind my head and shaking it in the direction of "Hell no." I didn't feel nervous, but I had my guard up. He took me for lunch to a small fish & chips restaurant. It was also a high school hang out, since they had video games. He brought me there, expecting to run into some of his buddies, so we could join them after our meal. After we ate, played a couple games and interacted with his friends, hours went by and the sun was setting. I informed him that I needed to get home, so we said our goodbyes and walked over to his parent's van. Right before he opened the door, he leaned in for a kiss. That one kiss sent chills down my spine, and I didn't want it to end. Eventually, we ended up in the rear of the van, but I didn't allow him to proceed past first base (which meant no further than touching breasts). Now, at this point I had been gone all day and into early evening, so I dashed into the restaurant and called my mom from their payphone. When she answered, I started to explain why I was running late, but she interrupted me in mid-sentence; and said, "Your father had a severe stroke."

At Fourteen and Feeling like Doomsday

It was the year in 1982; Mom rushed us to the hospital since my dad's health deteriorated from the stroke. We had to drive to Virginia, because that's where he was working for the period of time. The entire ride I remained silent, with thoughts whirling around in my head. It was over three years without communication between us, consequently, a complete outsider. I was concerned, but then again, my heart felt empty. When we arrived at the hospital, I was not eager to remove myself from the vehicle, but Mom's support guided me through the anguish. While I was walking down the hallway in the direction of his room, I could feel my stomach churning and started breathing heavily. The whole situation felt uneasy and my body sought to spin around and disappear, but before I had the chance, my grandmother walked out from his hospital room and squeezed me tight. The atmosphere was somber, like he already died and the family was mourning. Only one person was allowed in his room, so my grandmother motioned for me to proceed forward, so I slowly opened the door and peaked around the corner. When I glanced in his direction, he was completely unrecognizable because of all the tubes surrounding him along with the ventilator helping him breathe. Lying there in a state of coma, he was unaware I was present, but I walked over and looked downward upon his emotionless body. Still having mixed feelings, I took his hand, advised him of my presence, expressed my concern, and wishing him a full recovery. I walked out of the room baffled by mix of emotions regarding this individual I barely knew anymore; nevertheless, he was my dad.

The next day they airlifted him to a hospital in Pennsylvania, closer to his home. We had just driven to Virginia; therefor Mom was contemplating on whether she wanted to drive another four hours to the transferred hospital. After conversing with grandma on the phone, she decided it was substantial because his health has not improved overnight. The minute we arrived at the hospital the whole family was sitting in the waiting room. I was delighted to see them all, even if it was under these circumstances, and then embraced each one before I entered his room. He looked the same as yesterday, but this time, they had his hands tied to the bed railings for safety reasons. After I had my brief visit, I walked out of the room feeling emotionless, just like I did previously. When I looked toward the family, they were sobbing and hugging one another, but I couldn't shed one tear. Before departing the hospital, I said goodbye, and then embraced each family member before walking down to the lobby, where my mom was waiting for us. After we arrived in the lobby, immediately, my sisters and I stopped dead in our tracks because Mom was talking intently to an unfamiliar female and her young daughter. We slowly walked over with confusion written all over our face, and then Mom introduced us to our half-sister, which she kept the secret until now. Her name was Tonya. On the way home, my sisters and I were traumatized by what just transpired. Now that the secret was out, Mom explained the entire situation regarding Tonya; she was the daughter of our dad, disowned from a previous marriage before their own relationship. The day couldn't get any worse as I felt my world caving in. I was in total disbelief that Dad gave up his parental rights to his precious daughter. I went through every emotion possible during the journey home, which completely drained the little life out of me. I spent the rest of the night lying in the bedroom trying to comprehend my dad's actions, along with how Tonya will fit into our lives.

Dad's Miraculous Recovery and Secrets

A week went by and my dad made a miraculous recovery, except that he was paralyzed on the right side along with speech impediment. After going through months of rehabilitation, his speech impediment improved and walk slowly with a limp; unfortunately, his arm never regained sensation. With his disabilities, he needed around the clock assistance, so my grandma had made a tough decision and put him in a group home, which takes care of other individuals with disabilities. At forty years old, his life completely changed forever. After becoming acclimated with his new way of living, my mom would drive us there several times to visit. It was definitely awkward as the stranger still lingers within, but the sorrow overpowers the strangeness with his new circumstances. I looked toward the bright side, and recognized the positiveness of his life-threatening illness; gaining an additional sister. Periodically, when Tonya would visit, the conversations among ourselves involved the similarities between both our moms with Dad's abusive behavior. Apparently, he was always a narcissistic, abusive jerk, up until now.

Not soon after learning, I had a new sister, another surprise showed up at our front door. The entire family was home at the time, which is very rare, and I heard a knock at the front door. I walked over, peaked out the window, because we weren't expecting anyone at the time; a strange man appeared standing there waiting patiently. I yelled for Mom advising her about the guest at the front door. After she opened it and took one glance, instantly she slammed the door in his face. When she turned around, her face was the color of a tomato and the vein in the middle of her far head popped out; which means, get out of her way, hell is going to break loose. Knowing that look, my heart started pounding, and I wanted to run for my life. The scared feeling vanished when I realized it wasn't my misconduct, but anxious regarding the stranger. She made my sisters and I proceed to our bedrooms and close the doors. Even though the situation wasn't regarding myself, I was scared because of the hostile environment I just left behind. What felt like a lifetime, was only an hour, when I was able to come out from our bedroom.

Mom gathered us around the kitchen table, so she can explain everything that emerged. My mom's red face, now turned into splotches as her nerves were subsiding, but still shaking over the situation. She had problems speaking, as the words wouldn't come out of her mouth, so Colleen started the conversation. Colleen (who was aware of her paternal dad) informed us that over many years of researching, she ultimately found him. They corresponded with one another by writing letters. Colleen said, she kept it a secret because she knew how Mom would react, exactly the way she did when he appeared unannounced. Doreen and I were never informed that Colleen had a separate Dad, so now, once again; I'm in complete disbelief! Mom glanced over and saw the appalling look on our faces and decided to finally speak out loud on the subject of the matter. Mom explained her whole life story, and how she became pregnant with Colleen at the age of fifteen. The parents forced them to marry, then ultimately divorced, and he gave up his parental rights with Colleen. After listening, I completely understand why Mom was pissed when he appeared and slammed the door in his face! I remained seated, with questions swirling in my head, but then kept silent since it had been a long emotional day for all of us. Instead, I went back to my room and pondered regarding this secret that was just revealed. Life was definitely challenging me with emotions that I never knew existed, because I spent most of my childhood shutting down the world and hiding inside.

The family was getting back to normalcy since all the secrets were revealed. Colleen graduated high school, I remained hormonal boy crazy, and Mom never dismissed dating; given that she met a cowboy at the Winners Circle Saloon. Well, I personally presumed a wannabe cowboy, because when she brought him home, I was expecting an entirely different prospect. A Tom Selleck or Sam Elliott appearance, from their cowboy characters in movies, visualized in my mind.

After getting acquainted with his non-cowboy appearance, for no apparent reason, this feeling of peace rushed all throughout my body while he stood inside our home. This gentleman was of average height, salt and pepper colored hair, curls, and a mustache that matched the color of his hair. Mom introduced us; he was very soft spoken, but had this boyish twinkle in his eyes. With the short introduction we had, before heading out on their date, I sensed, he was very genuine with his desires to acquire all information regarding our interests. In that moment, remembering all the men she dated, this gentleman may perhaps blend into our family perfectly.

As my mom's relationship progressed, so did my frame of mind. He was certainly remarkable in every way, which made me elated to have him join our family. He had expressed how authentic a father figure was destined to be. I not only gained a wonderful Step Father, in addition, step-sisters and brother too.

Emotionally Evolving

My views on relationships had changed since my step-father came into our lives. The chaos had subsided, and I could feel the insecurities diminish within.

The following summer of 1983, I was fifteen; rode my bicycle to Karina's house to spend the afternoon. I refuse to stay at home during any length of time in the summer, because it was torturous to live in Timbuktu and pretend to be mimes so Mom could sleep; she was still on night shift. I put a great deal of miles on my bicycle and was in the best shape; I should have joined a bike-a-thon. After relaxing in her living room, drinking coke and watching soap operas, we both decided to ride our bicycles into Turkey Hill Mini-mart for goodies. I thought to myself, what's another mile after I just rode five to her home, I was in fit condition. After our arrival, we parked our bicycles alongside the ones previously there. As we approached the doors to proceed inside, two good-looking boys were leaving. Everyone glanced at each other, and nodded our heads hello. While wandering around the store, hitting one another and giggling, as we read each other's minds, both boys were adorable and our type. The one boy had curly blonde shoulder length hair while the other had short dark brown that was parted in the middle. The boys appeared to be in shape because they had muscular legs. Trying to keep an eye on every move they made and picking out a snack, I felt like a private investigator, trying to catch someone in action. We rushed in line to pay for our snacks and ran outside so we could introduce ourselves. We came to a complete halt, as they were standing by their bikes next to ours. The conversation went effortlessly between us; in fact, I don't recall one awkward moment the entire time. They asked if we wanted to join them on their bike ride back to their hometown, and we both agreed in unison! Again, thinking, what's another three miles to my daily workout. Our destination ended up at a theater complex, where we spent most of the afternoon sitting on benches conversing. Since, we had been gone for quite some time; all of us used the payphones to check-in with our parents, which informed us to start heading home. Before we peddled away, the blonde boy walked over and asked for my phone number. Even though he wasn't my type, I provided it to him. Our day turned out completely opposite with the intentions of both getting lucky, but that didn't discourage Karina.

 The very next day, I received a phone call, and therefor arranged for him to visit. He was also fifteen without a driver's license, so he rode his bicycle, which was approximately eight miles one way. I was very impressed with his fit physique! The day went exceptionally well, since we occupied our time playing video games and walking around outdoors conversing. After dinner, he leaned in for an incredible kiss and rode off into the sunset. The relationship lasted roughly two weeks when he ended it. I wasn't emotionally distraught since we barely knew each other, but then again, wished the relationship didn't end abruptly. Not even ten minutes after the break-up the phone rang again. I picked up the receiver; thinking maybe, my ex-boyfriend had a change of heart, but turned out to be his best friend. The same friend I met at Turkey Hill Mini Mart. After he introduced himself on the phone, it turned into complete silence. I was utterly thrown back, since his best friend literally just broke up with me. There was awkwardness and disbelief that lasted throughout the conversation, since he disregarded the fact of what just occurred between his best friend and I, but then, asking me out on a date? Politely, I said no, and explained how bizarre that would be after dating his best friend. His persistence landed him a date; Purple Rain was playing in the movie theaters at the time, and that would be the introduction of my first love.

    Between the age of fifteen and sixteen, sex was the only thing girls talked about. I can't speak for anyone else's parents, but my mom never provided the sex conversation. I don't recall the school having a class on sexual education, so therefore, I learned all about sexual intercourse vicariously through friends. Whenever we had a conversation about sex, excitement arose because the lack of awareness and expectations.

Sweet Sixteen

When I turned sixteen, Mom had a surprise party for me at the house. I walked in the front door and everyone in the living room sprang upwards and screamed surprise! There were balloons and streamers decorating the house, plus a gigantic happy birthday banner taped on the wall. I was in total disbelief to witness how many friends that appeared in order to celebrate my birthday, along with my boyfriend. I had such gratitude toward my mom and friends for arranging a miraculous party that will be remembered forever.

First "Real" Boyfriend

My boyfriend graduated early from a different high school, as he was exceptionally smart, but didn't pursue college. By this time, we're dating about a month and our relationship started becoming exceptionally emotional. We didn't engage in sex, but became awfully close. Close enough where my mom sensed the bond forming, and told me to get on some contraceptives, so I wouldn't get pregnant. This was her one and only sex conversation. The following week, I took the written exam and driver's tests; passed them both. I traveled straight to the health clinic for birth control, and the doctor informed me that I shouldn't have sexual intercourse for at least a month without any kind of protection as I could get pregnant.

    The time had ultimately arrived, and mixed emotions came flooding to the surface. There were countless conversations regarding friends that have lost their virginity, and explained how hurtful the first time could be, but they were delighted to have their cherry popped (slang they used for breaking of the hymen). The anticipation was overwhelming, because of the curiosity of the feeling but frightened of bleeding during sex, to me that's disgusting. It was a date night on Friday, and he took me to a lovely restaurant. During our meal, the conversation arose regarding sexual intercourse, and he inquired if I was ready, thinking that was very sweet to have asked, instead of being presumptuous. I nodded my head yes, but quietly, I enquired about the location since both families were home. He leaned forward and replied, "I know the perfect place." In my mind, I was confident he knew more than one, because he wasn't a virgin. After dinner, we continued driving around curvy countryside roads, as if he was going in the direction of my house, but by-passed the road I normally proceeded on. As we're riding in the car endlessly, the anticipation became unbearable, until he eventually turned onto a stone road, which led us into the enormous forest. It was pitch black, so it made it difficult to see your surroundings. Right before he parked, I was able to glance over and read the fine print on the sign "State Game Lands." As soon as he turned off the engine, he pulled me closer, and immediately started kissing me, but I backed away because I was horrified. I sternly advised him, there was no way in hell; I was going to have sex in this tinker size car, and besides, what if someone catches us. Before I had a chance to say another word, he pulled me onto his lap and started caressing my body.

    Everything I was anxious about dissipated as the heat rose between us. It was like being in a sauna with the windows fogged and sweat dripping down our naked bodies. It didn't feel awkward, as he led the way, since I was the virgin. The position we were in was perfect for what was going to happen subsequently, there was a slight twinge, nothing unmanageable, and then it was done. Immediately, I turned on the light, took a big sigh of relief, because there wasn't a speck of blood left behind, which had been my worst nightmare. He turned on some music, and laid back in the front seats until the steam on the windows disappeared; then all of a sudden, there was a knock on the window.

Both of us, frantic, trying to get at least one piece of clothing on before he winds down the window, and then overheard the police officer's voice demanding him to step out of the vehicle. He had enough time to pull up his trousers minus underwear before proceeding forward. My heart was pounding and body trembling while the police officer was questioning him. It seemed as though he was outside forever, and I was frightened that he would get arrested. Then the officer walked over to the passenger side of the vehicle where I was seated. At this point, my bra and underwear were on, but I didn't have a chance to fully dress. He tapped on the window, I slowly cranked it down, and said, "Hello, officer." He pointed his flashlight down onto my face which was blinding, so I tried to shield my eyes from the light while conversing.

At this point, I thought I was having a heart attack; when he said, "Ma'am, are you all right?"

He repeated the same question three times, to make sure I was truthful, and each time I replied, "Yes, officer."

After the police officer realized, I wasn't being raped or held against my will, he let us go with a warning, but informed both of us that he had better not catch us here again. On the way home, I was completely speechless; as I was pondering over what transpired and perplexed, because losing my virginity wasn't what I envisioned and seemed overrated.

Starting Employment

After turning sixteen, I started looking around for employment. My grandparents provided me with Dad's car since he was disabled, so I needed gas money, in addition, automobile insurance. I filled out an application with Friendly's Ice Cream

Parlor as a waitress, but I never received a phone call. Not letting that discourage me, I walked into McDonald's, filled out their application. And two days later, I received a phone call for an interview. The day approached, I wore something nice, per Colleen's instructions and arrived on time for the interview. I felt confident with a touch of nerves, but stayed calm, answered all their questions, and they hired me on the spot. They handed me their brown polyester uniform and then I strolled out the double doors. Feeling a sense of accomplishment, I cranked up the music and smiled the entire way home.

Most of my sophomore year in high school consisted of working, attending parties, and dating on again and off again boyfriend. Our relationship turned tumultuous, because I caught him cheating and lies regarding his deception. With me being young and naïve, I agreed to take him back. The majority of time together was hostile instead of peaceful, but I struggled with relinquishing the first time "love," as it felt like the end of the world. The entire family was exhausted pertaining the drama between us. One evening we were arguing on the telephone, therefore, Mom barged into the room, grabbed the phone out of my hand, and disconnected the line. I stampeded out of the room, face beat red, and raised my voice towards her. I then became flabbergasted, because the last time, she soaped my mouth for being disrespectful. By looking at her demeanor, there wasn't remorse from her actions; in fact, she demanded we break up. When that flew out of her mouth, all hell broke loose. Our fight became profound; eventually, I advised her that I was leaving, and the response; I'll help pack your bags. After I ran into my bedroom, threw some clothes in a backpack; I started walking out of the house, and she blocked me only because she wanted my car keys.

It was a dark drizzly night, when I walked towards my boyfriend's house; which was roughly a seven miles hike. Tears rolled down my face for most of the journey, as I was distraught from what occurred, and Mom letting me walk alone in the darkness without knowing the destination. Getting closer to his home, the sadness quickly turned to fury because at this point, I felt unloved and uncared for. She didn't deserve knowing my destination. Fortunately, no one attempted to kidnap me, as I made it to his house safely. I noticed his car wasn't in the driveway, but knocked on the door anyway. When his mom opened it, she motioned for me to come inside and advised he'll be home any minute. She didn't question how I arrived or carrying bags, but she allowed me to sit down in silence until he arrived. The minute he walked through the back door, he noticed the emotional distress I was displaying, and wrapped his arms around me. He took my hand, and I followed him into his bedroom. I explained the entire situation and the ultimatum Mom commanded, which is why I departed. After discussing the condition with his parents and pleading, they agreed I could stay there for a few days, but I needed to sleep in his sister's bedroom. During the time I spent there, there was no communication with Mom, but she made sure I was safe. The weekend ended, and it was time to move forward, per his parent's request. I wasn't emotionally prepared to encounter Mom, so I called my best friend Karina. She discussed the circumstances with her parents, and they welcomed me into their home without time boundaries. Throughout the week at their home, Karina's dad would patiently discuss the situation with me. I sat there listening intently, as he had valid points aimed at equal parties. Being a doctor of psychiatry, he knew just how to reason with his patients. I became emotionally stronger from our discussions and moved back home.

Not long after the chaos involving Mom, a couple friends and I traveled to the shopping center. After we parked the car and proceeded to walk in the direction toward the shopping center, I glanced over and noticed my boyfriend's car. Thinking to myself, how bizarre, because he was supposed to be working. Out of curiosity, I walked over toward his vehicle, and when I approached it, he came around from the passenger side door engaged with a strange female. I exchanged some unpleasant words, but then, a sense of release flowed through my body, because I captured his deception. Witnessing his dishonesty, I found the strength to end our relationship.

I wish there would have been a book, or maybe there was, but didn't realize it; explaining the different steps on how to move forward from your first love break up; because I really could have used the advice. It was extremely heartbreaking, and I tried to diminish my emotional agony by drinking excessively or smoking marijuana until the next guy in my life showed up.

Dating an Officer

I was seventeen at the time, and working the drive-thru at McDonalds. After taking this guy's order, he pulled around to the pickup window in his police cruiser. I was focused toward getting the orders correct during rush hour that I never peeked inside the vehicle. As I was facing down taking another order, I opened the window and placed my hand outside to collect the money. I quickly gathered the change and grabbed his bag of food, only then I glanced inside the police car, and my heart skipped a beat. With his dark hair and mesmerizing eyes, I fell in love at first sight. I was anxious, but came across unruffled as I handed him his food. We exchanged words, and I must have verbalized something senseless, since the subject caused him to giggle before driving away. I felt an instant connection, but dismissed the emotion, because he was a police officer and I was a high school student. Weeks went by; it was a Friday night, and I was working the late shift in the drive-thru. It was practically closing time when the customer came into the drive-thru with their order, and when his car came around the corner, my heart skipped a beat and legs went limp; the gorgeous police officer was pulling up to the drive-thru window. During this moment, there were no customers waiting behind his car, and I wasn't occupied, automatically my flirty personality arose, and it converted into a pleasant conversation. In the role of a police officer and watching for safety, he asked me if the manager on duty walks us to our vehicles after closing time. The response I advised him was no, but our parking area wasn't far from the building, as I'm pointing in the direction to my Volkswagen blue Rabbit. He recommended for me to be careful, and drove off with his food. It had been a while since our last encounter, so I assumed the officer wasn't interested, or he would have asked me on a date. One late evening, I was speeding home because I had a junior license, which meant curfew was midnight. I came up to the four-way intersection, ignored the stop sign, made the right-hand turn, and spotted a police car parked on the side of the street with his lights turned off. My first response was, oh shit, he's going to pull me over in front of my house and hand me a ticket. I'm now past curfew, and I ran a stop sign. I proceeded to turn into the driveway, and when I emerged from the vehicle; the police cruiser pulled up behind me. It was dark outside, so I really couldn't observe the police officer's face, until he addressed me. My heart started pounding for different reasons now, because it happened to be the gorgeous man from the McDonald's drive-thru. Joking around, I said, are you stalking me? His smile was contagious, which revealed his perfect pearly white teeth. He bounced back with a response, "You're late and ran a stop sign."

I went to bed in disbelief, but ecstatic because he asked me out on a date! Getting our schedules together was almost impossible, plus Mom wanted to meet him; we finally collaborated a plan, and he arrived for dinner, then went for a run. It was a strange first date, but I felt ecstatic throughout the evening. The maturity of the relationship was completely different from what I was accustomed to during my last boyfriend. Mom was lenient with our relationship because she admired him; and allowed me to spend the night at his apartment during the weekends, or else she invited him camping with the family. The age difference interfered with our relationship, only when he was out drinking at bars, instead of spending time together.

Dating a police officer around my jurisdiction had its benefits; but also caused hatred toward me, with several high schoolers. One boy that lived down the road, organized a massive party while their parents were absent. He published flyers and handed them out to the students, and placed them on car windshields. I planned on showing my appearance, until my boyfriend advised not to attend, because he would be one of the officers apprehending them for underage drinking.

I had concealed the invasion, and therefore, left my friends stranded. The night of the party, I sat outside on the wooden deck feeling hopeless, and watched the police cruisers going past one by one. Monday morning, I went to school and noticed the glares toward me; everyone thought I blabbed, and pretended I didn't exist. Most of the students were acquaintances, not friends, but I felt the tension among the entire class. The following weekend, in the middle of the night, pumpkins and other debris were thrown on my deck for retaliation. My boyfriend arrived to inspect the damage and took photographs. A day or so later, he caught the suspects who caused the destruction. The boys were required to apologize to our family and obtained a fine. My popularity spiraled downhill, and they never invited me to another party while dating him. My demeanor came off indifferent, because I was absolutely in love with this man. One day after school, I was visiting my boyfriend at the police station; and as we're conversing, my home address came over the CB radio as an emergency. I started panicking, he bolted out the door while shouting toward me not to follow, until he investigates. Of course, I didn't pay attention, and drove extremely fast in order to arrive home. As I pulled up, there was an ambulance parked beside his patrol cruiser in front of my grandparent's home. Immediately, I sprinted inside, and noticed my grandfather, laying on the gurney, ready to be taken to the hospital. He had an acute stroke and wasn't completely coherent. After spending a week in the hospital, he came home with rigorous speech impediment caused from the stroke. He would have to write down his sentences as he couldn't speak properly. Sometimes, he would try to communicate, except the words wouldn't come out accurately or didn't have the patience, and it frustrated him to the point where, he would throw up his hands and walk away.

  My senior year was approaching and my boyfriend and I broke up; plus, I was in disarray with what to pursue after graduation, since I didn't have any interests.

  I was in total disbelief when we broke up, because the electricity between us was electrifying. I may have been in high school but I could have seen a future between us. There were problems, like any normal couple, but nothing major to the extent of breaking apart. I was absolutely in love; the devastation felt like a knife straight through my heart. Then to make matters worse, immediately he started dating another female, which we had courses together. Every time I strolled into class, jealousy shot through my body, which made it hard to concentrate on the lesson, the teacher was presenting. Eventually, over time, I was able to push through the loss and move on with my life. It happened to be the end of junior year when the guidance counselor invited me into his office, to discuss colleges that I may be interested in attending, or wanted to know the direction beyond high school. I shrugged my shoulders because I was completely at a lost. I was not the best scholar, since I had no interest in school, therefore, I never really attempted. The business courses I acquired throughout high school, was useless to me, as I had no attention in using skills that were taught.

    I pondered most of the senior year in high school regarding my future interests and I came to the conclusion that I wanted to travel around the world. I started researching trade schools with that kind of curriculum, and came upon a seven-month program in Travel & Tourism, located in Pittsburgh, PA named Wilma Boyd. The trade school provided interviews throughout the program, to position you in the work force. Although, you must pass all your curriculum in order to obtain the employment, after being hired. One of my best friends Sara, decided to follow the same footsteps, and we're ecstatic to see where this journey leads us.

Adulthood

I graduated from high school June 1987 and after graduation, my parents bought a home in Hershey, PA. The house had enough rooms to accommodate my grandparents as well; my grandfather's health was deteriorating, not only from the stroke, but had lung cancer. In July, we relocated into our 1940 cape cod style home, which had white siding and green shutters. The design on the inside of the home was converted into two apartments with one front door entrance, in addition, two separate entryways to each apartment. Our family (minus Colleen since she relocated to Washington DC) lived in the upstairs apartment and my grandparents were on the first floor. My parents placed me in a room that had a kitchen sink and cupboards; which was the smallest room in the entire house, (especially when you put normal sized bedroom furniture inside). Although, the best part of my "cubicle," was crawling through the window and sun tanning on the roof.

    I worked at a couple diverse employments throughout school, but after relocating, I started working for the Hershey Chocolate Company's storage warehouse. The hourly pay was remarkable and a seasonal position, which was perfect, since I was departing for tourism school in the fall. I packaged all types of chocolate bars and hard candy into boxes, but devoured more than I packed.

    Boyfriends became non-existent, since I was single throughout senior year in high school, and summertime before heading to tourism school. I maintained contact with both ex-boyfriends but it wouldn't go further than sexual activity. I wanted additional from the policeman, as I was still in love with him; but I accepted his actions, within hopes the relationship would rekindle.

    Even though, over the recent years, my family became established and peaceful environment, I struggled inside, with my self-worth. Any kind of emotions that would surface, I immediately shut them out. That's how I coped with visiting Dad periodically, at his disabled home environment. With all the distress, and harm he caused our family, I made the feelings dormant. Adapting to my new normal progressed into living like a chameleon; I was able to weave through different human beings without them knowing what truly lies within.

September came like the speed of lightning, and the time had come to depart for school. Living on my own, brought excitement within, which I haven't felt in quite some time. Our housing wasn't the normal dorms in college. They were one-bedroom high-rise apartments, which slept four, with two single beds in the living room and two in the bedroom on Duquesne University's campus. We had a friend from high school that was attending Duquesne, so it was pleasant having someone familiar close by. We would party together, along with another group of schoolboys that were acquaintances attending a different college nearby. Sara and I started out with two other roommates, but one of them departed within the first month of school due to homesickness. The other roommate was extremely obnoxious from the Bronx, therefor we had to accept her boldness, but not when she prevented others from sleeping, due to quarreling with her boyfriend on the telephone. I became acclimated with the school fairly quickly and enjoyed the majority of professors. During the week, Sara and I explored Pittsburgh when we didn't have classes, and frequently partied in our dorms. The weekends were a whole different story, that's when foolishness came swarming in. Each weekend was pack full and consisted of concerts (we received back stage passes to meet the musicians in Whitesnake), going to NFL football games, enjoying the nightclub life (we acquired fake ID's), and relishing the moment among friends from high school. They had a vehicle, so they would come and pick us up, and take us back to their dorm to party and spend the evening.

Through the duration of school, I didn't find it necessary to obtain girlfriends, but gained a boyfriend that I met in a nightclub. He was definitely my type; tall, dark and handsome, and smelled astounding from his cologne. He lived in the Pittsburgh area with his family, and would spend the weekends accompanying me, until an abrupt scuffle happened involving him and a friend from high school. The altercation was excessive, by the way, of my boyfriend's demeanor, which caused hardships among Sara and boyfriends from high school, since I wouldn't dismiss our relationship.

The school year came to a completion, and I only attended one job interview with Eastern Airlines as a flight attendant. They flew me to Atlanta Georgia for two interviews, and the second interview they critiqued the way my hair was French braided. I remember flying home, astounded, with the interviewers for berating my hair appearance; I wasn't surprised, when I was turned down for the position. I wouldn't have accepted it anyway after their unprofessionalism, and besides, the only reason I applied, was because they hired Sara. Obviously, the position was not meant to be at the time.

For the first time in my life, I was an academic scholar, since I completed the program with the best results in each class. I proved to myself that I was worthy and intelligent after utilizing the time and efforts into my studies. Since I didn't have a career lined up, I moved back home and filled out applications for travel agent positions. In the meantime, while researching for employment, I traveled to Pittsburgh on weekends to visit my boyfriend. The relationship lasted a month or so after my return home, but then again, extended distance never survives in relationships; at least ours certainly didn't. Neither of us were extremely wounded with the situation, as we weren't in love with one another.

Big Girl Jobs

Soon, I was hired on the spot for a Travel Agent position that was located in downtown Harrisburg. Unfortunately, the owner was an alcoholic, which affected his ability to run the office properly, so he eventually had to shut down the agency. I may have only worked there for four months, but found a best friend, Lorraine, during the short amount of time working together.

During the process of the previous agency closing, Lorraine and I were informed from the owner that a new travel agency was opening across the street, in the Strawberry Square Mall. Both of us applied for the positions; immediately, they hired us along with three other employees. The company was recognizable, since they had agencies all around the world. We were hired as corporate agents and sat in the rear of the office and managed all travel requests from contracted corporate companies. It became swift pace with receiving phone calls constantly, which I enjoyed, because it made the time go by faster. The entire advantage of working for a larger travel agency was higher pay, health insurance, retirement savings, and the opportunity to earn free travel. Starting a career with this agency, I could afford to purchase a new vehicle. I loved the old Honda Prelude that I owned, but now, I could afford and deserved a newer version; so, I drove myself to the Honda dealership. I took one glance at the sticker price of a new Prelude, and contemplating whether or not I wanted to put myself in debt over a car. Eventually, without any assistance from my mom during this experience, I walked out with a brand new two-door Honda CRX sports car. I assume I was an easy target, a young female and I didn't finagle; but it was the principle of getting approved for my first loan and being independent. The reason I attended travel school was finally coming to fruition, as I started traveling around the world. Growing up, the farthest place we ever vacationed was Orlando, Florida, to visit Disney World. Being able to travel and experience the different cultures, took it to a whole new level, as now, I recognized I was born to travel. I would be looking into the next vacation, after a vacation. We would take all means of transportation, not just airplanes.

Encountering Boyfriend within Travel Experiences

One weekend, Lorraine and I, decided to take a journey on Amtrak from Harrisburg to Boston. A friend of ours that we met in Toronto, Canada, was going to be in Boston for the weekend. Whenever we traveled together, the shenanigans arose which kept our trips interesting. We were very sociable and enjoyed encountering different individuals, and staying in touch. I was under the legal age for drinking, but I had another individual's driver's license; the picture on the license resembled nothing like me, but the bouncers and bartenders never questioned it. The train ride consisted of countless hours to get to our destination, since they had multiple stops in between states, to allow other passengers onboard. One of the stops was New York City and a group of passengers stepped aboard, traveling to their own destination. I noticed this particular gentleman who picked a seat diagonal from me, and continued looking towards my direction. I must have appeared freezing, (which I was) so he offered his leather jacket in order for me to stay warm. I accepted his kindness and we started conversing, continuously until his destination, which was Rhode Island, where his family resided. As I returned the leather jacket before he departed, he requested for my phone number. Lorraine and I thought he was handsome, and his persona drew my attention. Majority of the weekend, I questioned whether or not he would actually call me; but I dismissed the emotions, and we had an astounding visit with our friend from Canada. We had walked around the entire city exploring Quincy Market and visiting different bars, especially Cheers, since it was one of my favorite shows on television. When I walked down the steps into the bar, immediately I was disappointed; the layout was not the same from the television set. In fact, it was so small you could barely move and was divided into sections. Even though we immediately departed without having a beer, I was pleased to experience Cheers, but I had no desire to revisit. Unfortunately, the weekend ended and we said farewell to our friend from Canada in hopes, we shall see him again.

    After I arrived home, there was a message on the answer machine, from the stranger on the train. I instantly dialed his phone number, and he requested that I visit him in New York City. Without thinking twice about the possible danger, I could have faced, I accepted, and drove into New York City the following weekend. I arrived at his place of employment, the same time his day ended, and then drove to his apartment. We barely made it through the front door without the heat of passion, caressing my body, kissing hard, and stripping. He scooped me up, and carried me into the bedroom. I typically don't have sexual interactions involving someone I barely know, but it seemed natural, and I couldn't resist the Latin lover since he was from

Columbia. He showed me around New York City, went to the movies, and spent time conversing with his colleague. By the end of the weekend, we were both astonished with how our relationship transpired quickly, and we molded into a couple right away. It was difficult to depart, and watch his expression before driving home, as our connection seemed surreal. Our long-distance relationship succeeded for a while and consisted of taking turns visiting both our homes. Luckily, at this point, my grandparents relocated in their own apartment since my grandfather's health was stable, and I was able to move into their old bedroom along with a new double bed. Having privacy during his visits I felt was a necessity.

Intro to the Mafia

Our relationship went up another level when he wanted to introduce me to his family. As we were driving to Rhode Island for a visit, he informed me, that none of his family spoke English, only Spanish, except his sister. When we arrived, I instantly felt uncomfortable and unsuitable, because being surrounded by individuals and not able to communicate was agony. I couldn't understand any of their conversations amongst themselves. During the entire visit, I was perplexed, because my boyfriend never offered to translate, until our conversation on the way home; seemingly, his dad was in the mafia. Only then, it made sense why everything was so secretive while visiting. Not only was his dad in the mafia; apparently, my boyfriend was also; but was permitted to disconnect from the gang. As we drive home, I tried to evaluate the circumstances; but I have seen mafia movies, and there is no chance, you could release without being murdered. Therefor he's lying, or the Mafia changed the guidelines; which is highly unlikely. I never brought up the subject again, as I really didn't want to be involved. Unfortunately, as rapidly as the relationship began; it suddenly came to a halt, after his corporation dismissed him. While speaking on the telephone, he didn't go into detail regarding the circumstances; but advised me they didn't need his Paralegal services any longer. I didn't obtain more information as I figured he'd find employment from another corporation; on the contrary, he requested to borrow money. I didn't attain a savings account, as I just began working for a new travel agency, and having a car payment; but turned out to loaning him $175.00. I was young and naïve, and believed his word in regards to paying the loan back; but instead, he abandoned me, without any explanation. After the separation, I called multiple times and left messages on the answering machine; but he never responded. What I wanted to accomplish was arrange a particular day, where I could arrive at his apartment to gather items I left behind, and collect the money he owed.

    Weeks went by, and there was no response; so, I took it upon myself, to drive there unexpectedly. After my arrival, I knocked on the front door and his colleague answered. Even though there was a confused expression on his face, he invited me inside. We relaxed in the living room, watching television and engaged in conversation, until the ex-boyfriend came home. I glanced at the clock, and it was after midnight when he finally strolled inside, holding hands and giggling with his girlfriend. When they walked into the living room, he glanced over and noticed me sitting on the couch; he looked stunned, but stayed calm, as he demanded the girlfriend go into his bedroom. He proceeded to sit beside me, and was questioning my intentions. Disregarding the fact, he instantly had a girlfriend after abandoning me which at this point, he was most likely unfaithful. He gathered my belongings, and informed me that he'll repay the loan, when he attains employment. I collected my belongings and was prepared to depart heartbroken, when his colleague snatched my keys and advised me, it's not safe to drive home this late; you can sleep on a cot in my bedroom. I thought to myself, there is no way in hell, I wanted to stay any longer than I had to, knowing he was in the other room having sexual encounters with his girlfriend, but I had no other options. I lay wide awake all night, distraught, but trying to comprehend his colleague's actions in making me stay. As soon as the sun started to rise, I ran out of there like a flash of lightning, without looking backwards. The entire drive home, I sobbed uncontrollably, I didn't realize how fast I was traveling, until I looked in my rear-view mirror and noticed the red and blue lights flashing. I pulled off to the side of the highway and the policeman walked up toward the window. He acknowledged how distraught I appeared, and questioned why I seemed so upset. I explained the entire situation; and apparently, he felt remorseful and left me proceed without a speeding ticket. After the encounter with the police officer, my emotions transformed quickly, because now I'm pissed off, of the outstanding money that I will never receive. Weeks went by, and he wouldn't return my phone calls regarding the unpaid debt. The money that vanished wasn't a setback, but it was the principle. Lorraine and I came to with a creative and hilarious idea. Out of construction paper, we made a loan coupon booklet, for installments until it's repaid, and mailed it to him. He had never acknowledged of receiving the booklet, and the money was gone forever.

Turning Legal at "Twenty-One"

The summer of 1989, and I became the legal drinking age of twenty-one. The anticipation and overwhelming excitement, because I'm finally legal to consume alcohol, without fake Identification, turned out to be boring. My birthday landed in the middle of the week, live music was non-existent during that time, and most of my best friends weren't legal. A few co-workers and friends that I met from the mall joined my celebration, which paid my check. Later in the evening, Mom joined the group and became my designated driver. I was also insulted, when we visited two bars, and none of the bouncers carded me. I was ultimately able to present my real ID, instead of the fake one, but never had the opportunity. The mixed drinks served that night, were extremely diluted, as I went home, without even a buzz. I lived the excitement of turning twenty-one, vicariously through my best friends; as each month, someone was becoming legal. At times, the celebration became out of control, where the drinking was excessive; and not just for the birthday girl, but also myself.

There's this one incident, I will never forget to this day because Karina will never let me live it down. I had two free airline tickets, so I asked her if she wanted to join me on a trip to Key West Florida, for the weekend. She wasn't twenty-one, but was able to get a fake identification from a friend. Our flight departed early Friday morning, but the night before, I went out to celebrate one of our friend's 21st birthday. We shut down the bar at two a.m., so I arrived home fairly late. The next morning the alarm didn't go off, or I slept through it; the only noise jolted me awake, was someone pounding on the front door and ringing the doorbell. I sprung out of bed, disoriented, as I was still drunk from three hours ago, and I stumbled toward the front door. When

I flung the door open, not realizing I was stark naked, and the disgusted face; I realized we missed our flight. Trying to get my bearings together on the situation, she advised me to get dressed. When I invited Karina inside to figure out a solution, I glanced over and noticed my pajamas laying on the couch. I had no recollection of placing them there, or why, because I normally wear them to bed, it must have been a good night, until we missed our flight.

After calling the airlines, and informing them a small tale as to why we missed our flight, they changed it to the following day, without penalty. The entire trip, we kept reminiscing and chuckling regarding me swinging the door open, naked without knowing who was present.

Till Death Do Us Part

The One

Periodically, when I came home from work, I noticed a Honda Prelude driving by the house. It looked exactly like the one I owned, but sold it to Doreen. The car wasn't the only thing that caught my eye, it was the attractive gentleman driving the vehicle too, and wondering where his destination may be, as he zips by.

In the meantime, after acknowledging this attractive man driving past, and inquisitive regarding his location; I kept myself entertained at our local bars, listening to music, since all my friends were twenty-one. One of our favorite bars, named Spanky's, offered $1 drink specials every Thursday, and live music performed toward the rear of the building with a tiny dance floor. We would gather together throughout happy hour; order countless drinks until their limit, and close down the bar. By closing time, the tabletop wasn't visible because of the stack of empty glasses sitting everywhere.

One particular Thursday in springtime of 1990, the night started out our normal routine, as we all met at Spanky's for happy hour; then I had unexpected surprise, eventually changed my life forever. When we walked through the entryway, a band was performing; the waitresses seemed overwhelmed, as it was difficult maintaining everyone's orders, and it was challenging maneuvering around individuals, since it was overly crowded. After we snatched a table and received our beverages, several of the women walked around the club in order to socialize and watch the band. I stayed behind, relaxing at our table and enjoying my beverage, when all of a sudden, my girlfriend Natalie approached the table elated, and advised me Daniel was standing with a group of friends located near the band. I was flabbergasted, because I haven't seen him, since the roller rink days when I was in elementary school. Hearing his name took me down memory lane because during that time, I thought he was cute but disliked his attitude; he acted too cool with that whistle around his neck. Working there definitely made him cocky, because every time I roller-skated past, he blew the whistle and advised me to slow down; even though I wasn't reckless!

After the quick flashback, I proceeded to follow her; trying to push my way through the crowd, until she pointed in the direction to where he was standing. I immediately stopped and looked around, but didn't recognize him, while I'm looking for the same appearance from when we were young. Natalie clutched my arm; like she was leading a horse to its trough, and guided me to his location. As we moved closer, I became speechless, at how his appearance completely changed, not surprised why I couldn't identify him. We graduated from the same high school, but he was three years older than I. The memory embedded in my head from his previous appearance was; short brown hair, parted in the middle, and feathered perfectly on both sides. I guarantee that he used hairspray, because his hair was never out of place.

He always sported skintight Levi jeans that showed off his buttocks. But, now, his appearance is the typical '90s hairstyle, where it's longer in the back and shorter on the sides, and hair changed black in color. I also noticed him wearing big round glasses, with a thinner build. I thought to myself, he's still attractive, even with the major changes in his appearance. When

I approached him, I couldn't stop smiling, and the only words I expressed was, "Do you remember me?" The alcohol could have had something to do with the lack of communication that stemmed from the mouth; but apparently, my appearance didn't change drastically, as he remembered exactly who I was. After our short conversation, I advised him it was nice seeing him again, and headed back to the table. I informed my friends about the introduction from hell I just encountered with Daniel, and one friend mentioned, her boyfriend must be present too, since they're best friends. During our conversation, the men happened to stroll over to the table, as they were preceding out the doors. Some of us, decided to follow them to another bar. After approaching the bar's entrance, some women meandered straight to the restroom including myself. As we're socializing and examining our hair in the mirror, one girlfriend swung the bathroom door open, all excited to reveal the fact, that Daniel was interested in taking me on a date.

Our First Date

We came out of the restroom, giggling over what just transpired and proceeded our way over to their table. I made sure to sit next to him and we immediately started reminiscing about the roller rink; only then, I informed him how annoying he was with his whistle. The awkwardness subsided, and turned out to be a very comfortable conversation. Eventually, before the night had ended, he asked me out on a date, for when he returns from New York City; and I accepted. The following week after rescheduling our date (I don't recall why we had to reschedule), he asked for my address, with the purpose of picking me up. After providing him my location, he started laughing, because his apartment was right down the road from my house above the vacuum cleaner store. He suggested cooking dinner and then travel to a nightclub, since a familiar band was performing. I replied perfect, and I'll walk down to your apartment. Date night arrived, and during preparation, there was a calm, comfortable feeling inside; which wasn't typical for my first dates. Usually, I would have butterflies in my stomach or feeling anxious.

Although, I didn't overthink this perception, since I previously knew him, I was eager for our evening together. When I strolled down to his apartment, there sat the Honda Prelude, I observed driving by my house. I felt completely flabbergasted; it was Daniel, and the mystery was solved! Immediately, as I proceeded up the steps, I smelled something delicious and when he opened the door, the aroma made my mouth water. He cooked an enormous pan of lasagna that could have fed the entire town. I was pretty sure he was a chef in another lifetime, because it was one of the best lasagna's, I have ever tasted. As we sat in the kitchenette, drinking wine and eating his delicious dinner our conversation seemed to flow the entire time. It was the same sensation I had felt previously; we're very comfortable around each other. We didn't notice the clock since we're enjoying each other's company; it was almost time for the band to perform. We quickly cleaned the kitchen and drove to the nightclub. As soon as we pulled into the parking lot, it occurred to me, that I forgot my driver's license. I was distressed, since I just ruined our date; he stayed calm and made alternate plans. With his quick thinking because there's nothing to accomplish without my ID, so we drove to Mt. Gretna, where he grew up. Mt. Gretna is a gorgeous summer destination for families with their cute cottages, large lake for swimming, hiking, fishing, cobblestone walkways, ice cream parlors, outdoor theater, shops, and it's all nestled in a wooded area. After departing the vehicle, we strolled around on the cobblestoned streets; gazing at the beauty of our surroundings while our conversation topics went into several different directions. By the end of the night, I think we discussed our entire lives, or maybe it felt that way, since we strolled for hours. After arriving back at my house, he was a complete gentleman leaning in for a sweet kiss, and asked me out on another date, except this time, with my driver's license. During the year of 1990, dating went exceptionally well; our communication was superb because we never kept our thoughts hidden. We were compatible in many ways, including the bedroom, although sexual activity wasn't the main focus within our relationship, therefore I disregarded the concern I once had. Eventually, we spent the majority of nights together, so in the end we resided as one.

Meeting His Parents

Over the winter, I flew into Erie, PA for the weekend, to meet his parents; since he was already there, visiting for the week. Instantly, I fell in love with their warm welcome as though I was part of the family. The only portion of visiting that I wasn't in favor of, was requiring to sleep in separate bedrooms, even though, we practically resided together. I released the frown on, as this could be exciting sneaking into each other's bedrooms while they're sleeping or finding time while they're working. During the entire weekend, it became nonexistent as he turned me down; stating he felt uncomfortable. I respected his feelings, but still disappointed.

I didn't experience many relationships before; but what I had learned from each one is, not every relationship is perfect, and you have to adapt to their desires and beliefs as well.

Step-Father Vanishing

Unfortunately, while my relationship was moving forward, my mom's life was turned upside down. My stepfather packed up his belongings while Mom worked the night shift, and left a letter requesting a divorce. Doreen caught him being unfaithful, but Mom didn't want to acknowledge it, until now. I felt heart ached for my mom, as this was the most decent gentleman she ever encountered; and truly loved. The devastation from losing someone you trusted, was agonizing for my mom and Doreen. Colleen was living in California starting her own family, and I didn't let the emotions arise as; I became accustomed to changing of the guards, with numerous men in and out during childhood. Mom had been mourning the passing of her sister from Multiple Sclerosis; now, she's required to face the single life again, and comprehend her father's lung cancer was worsening, which means limited survival time.

It was 1991, when my boyfriend asked for my hand in marriage. It wasn't a surprise engagement, since I had to select the engagement ring because he didn't trust his judgment regarding the style. One night while preparing dinner, when he got down on one knee, even though he was sick, and asked me to marry him. It was nothing elaborate, just a matter of fact; he desired for us to become one. Of course, I said yes! Both families and friends were elated when we revealed the engagement, but wasn't surprised, as our relationship was always solid. A couple months after the engagement, I received a phone call from my mom; letting me know, Pop-Pop (again that's what we called our grandfather) was in the hospital. His lung cancer metastasized, to the point where doctors couldn't assist any longer, other than keep him comfortable. When I rushed into the hospital to visit, he was extremely emotional from the morphine; he cried the entire visit. I tried to keep my composure, until he mentioned that he will no longer be living when I walk down the aisle. I no longer had control of the tears, as I was completely devastated and felt hopeless at watching this beautiful soul, slowly leave our family. The journey of our relationship blossomed into a flower, as he taught me love. This was shown in many different ways, which helped shed some light on all relationships. Even though, he may not be there for the wedding, he provided his blessing, and advised me, I'm marrying an amazing man. My grandfather left this world on Feb 26, 1991. After Pop-Pop passed away, my fiancé and I moved into a different apartment, not far, from where we previously lived. Daniels old apartment was deteriorating and the landlord wouldn't address the issues, so we decided to relocate.

During the year 1991, busy with wedding preparations, it's shocking how sudden occurrences, happen within a short amount of time, when you least expect it. I was released from employment because the company lost major corporate accounts; but fortunately, I was hired instantly from another travel agency, located around the corner. During every employment, I was orbiting around the vicinity, and not by choice because I liked stability.

Wedding Preparations

One day, during the weekend, after running errands for the wedding, we arrived at my mom's house, unannounced. When I proceeded through the front door, yelling her name, I noticed a companion seated by the kitchen table. I couldn't quite see whom it was until I strolled into the kitchen. It was her manager from Hershey Foods, which who unfortunately, just lost his wife to cancer. They would quarrel during work hours but friends outside their employment. When his wife was living and Mom's soon to be ex-husband was present; periodically, the two couples would dance to the country style music at the Winners Circle. After visiting and saying our goodbyes, immediately, I was aware their relationship would progress to more than just friends. You have two beautiful souls, consoling each other during hardship, and I was right; soon after, their relationship went to a whole new level. I never thought, Mom would find love again; but turned out to be a nice surprise. We became very close in the short amount of time him coming into our lives; I felt comfortable enough, and asked him to walk me down the aisle. With the wedding arriving rapidly, I felt it necessary for Daniel and I to advise my dad of the engagement. They had encountered a few times, throughout our dating; and even though, Daniel was aware of the circumstances from my childhood, he never questioned once, why I required him in my life. On occasion, I would visit Dad in his assisted living home. I felt it necessary, since he was still my dad; but the love was absent. The visits were brief because his brain, never recovered completely, from the stroke and he would become exhausted quickly. When we walked inside the home, I showed off my gleaming engagement ring, and he immediately, said congratulations, but emotionless. Then I nonchalantly, informed him of the invitation to the wedding; but Mom's boyfriend will be walking me down the aisle. I felt nervous advising him of the situation because I was taking away the special moment; of a father walking his daughter down the aisle. He didn't seem disappointed, since he responded okay; but I think the stroke damaged that side of the brain, because he's been emotionless with anything. I was saddened by our relationship; as I wished it was different, and he was able to walk me down the aisle. All I ever wanted was a normal loving bond between a father and daughter; but unfortunately, there's a void within, due to his previous actions. Putting my feelings aside, of not having my biological father walk me down the aisle, I was getting excited for my special day.

Our wedding party consisted of eight total, four bridesmaids and groomsmen. Neither of my sisters were able to partake in the wedding, so I asked four best friends. One canceled last minute, therefore I enquired another friend, even though it was embarrassing, but necessary because I didn't want to have an uneven party. The bridesmaid's dresses that I chose were lovely quarter length, satin fabric, and maroon in color with a bow on the side. There was black lace that covered the satin on the upper torso and had laced sleeves. Their dress shoes were dyed the same color as the dress, since they were visible. The guys reserved black tuxedos with maroon bow ties. I found the perfect wedding dress from the first bridal boutique we entered. It was a beautiful white colored silky fabric that showed the curves of my upper torso. The sparkled sequins that were embedded in the material had a unique curve around the breast area. The short sleeves had ruffles along with the lower part of the dress from the waist down to the long train. The neck and chest area were completely bare, which allowed me to wear a nice necklace, if I desired. I also found a sequin and beaded head-piece that matched the dress perfectly. I felt like a princess going to the ball, when I tried it on; it was absolutely stunning, and fit me perfectly! I booked the venue located at the Hershey Lodge, in one of their ballrooms, and a DJ from a radio broadcasting station I listened to. Mom was in charge of finding someone for the flower arrangements and creating the cake. Everything was falling into place; no other problems in organizing and planning for the big day, other than the one bump in the road, finding a new bridesmaid, which worked out. I booked the honeymoon, since I was the travel agent; and we decided to take a seven-night cruise to the Western Caribbean; on Norwegian Cruise Lines. I had introduced him to cruising on a short four day, the previous year, and he absolutely loved it; so, we decided to make this cruise longer. The cruise left a day after the wedding, which worked out suitably; as we were ready for a vacation, after all this planning for our special day. Before the ceremony, we had to follow through with Christian classes, in order to get married in the United Church of Christ. The questions became hysterical, because, even though we lived together; we noticed rather quickly, we weren't familiar with one another, according to the simplest questions. Each class, we laughed all the way home. We decided to get married in my grandmother's church and have our Reverend assist with the ceremony. The church was larger and the pews had velvet padding, which made it more comfortable for the elderly. The church was still United Church of Christ, just a different location. I mailed over two-hundred invitations, and received approximately one-hundred and twenty responses back, that will be attending our celebration in marriage.

Bridal Shower

Before the wedding, Karina, whom was the maid of honor, held an extravagant bridal shower at her parent's gorgeous home. The rooms were lavished with wedding decorations; along with a handmade purple-laced parasol, sitting on the table, surrounding the gifts. The food was prepared to perfection; and so were the deserts, that Karina's Mom prepared from scratch. The bridal party, close friends, and relatives gathered around the room; we played silly games and everyone observed while I open gifts. I received plenty of sexy lingerie, which caused Daniel to be excited!

Bachelorette Party

The last hurrah of being single, came the bachelorette party! Karina had the arranged gathering at her parent's gorgeous house once more. They built an addition to their home that included an expansive bar and a complete game room. The great room was perfect for the occasion she organized. All women in the wedding party and a couple dear friends arrived to celebrate. It was open bar with snacks, and pizza that was delivered. For such a small gathering, I can guarantee the entire neighborhood heard our enjoyment for the night to remember. Then, all of a sudden, someone knocked at the door. Everyone became anxious because it was a police officer, most likely from all the noise and loud music.

Karina opened the door, invited him inside, and then questioned, "Is there a problem officer?" At that moment, corny striptease music started playing, and he danced toward me! Obviously, the prank was on me, since at one time I dated a policeman. I couldn't contain myself while laughing enormously which produced tears and abdominal pain. While dancing he stripped away his entire uniform, and was wearing blue underwear with my name engraved, which he handed to me at the conclusion of his show. He wasn't attractive; not my type anyway, but could dance! Each and every one had an amazing time, enjoying the entertainment that was provided, along with their lap dances; so, we decided to invite him to join us at a local bar. He accepted and we danced the night away. The next morning, I awoke to a touch of wetness on the sheets. I however, was inebriated from the previous night, and could barely open my eyes; I started smacking the bed in order to feel where the leak was originating. After waking Daniel, and explaining our dilemma with the water-bed; I finally opened my eyes to realize, we didn't have a leak; I accidently peed on the bed.

The night before our wedding, we had rehearsal at the church, and then the entire party proceeded to dinner. After the rehearsal dinner, Daniel and I went our separate ways. He slept at his friend's house, while I stayed at the apartment; seeing as we followed the bad luck rule.

The Big Day

I awoke revived and considerably calm; as the preparations went extremely well throughout the year for our magnificent day. I had my makeup and hair professionally styled, and then drove toward the church. It was a beautiful spring sunny day; 80 degrees, and all the tulips and daffodils blossomed, along with the buds on the trees. My mom and bridesmaids were at the church, waiting for my arrival, while the men were across the street drinking shots. I carried an overnight bag with wedding gear inside along with a change of clothes for the overnight stay in the hotel, but forgot one particular item, deodorant. I was panicking, because I didn't want to cause a nasty aroma; especially since it's hot outside and no air conditioning in the church. We instantly called my hairdresser, and asked her if she wouldn't mind bringing one along to the church since she was coming to finish the touch-ups. With a big sigh of relief and applying the deodorant, I was ready to walk down the aisle.

Beginning a Family

My New Life

On May 2, 1992, I took my vows very seriously, as I didn't want to become my mom; married several times, in addition to a dysfunctional family. After the wedding and honeymoon too, life went back to reality, or so I thought until Daniel came home from work, and informed me, that we needed to relocate to Delaware, Ohio. Contel, the company he worked for, had been bought by GTE. His position was being eliminated in the Hershey, PA office; so, they were transferring him to Ohio.

At the moment, I was in disbelief; since we were newlyweds, and I had a decent job; but after the shock subsided my feelings altered, and I started looking forward to a new adventure. I never lived in another state before, consequently, it may be exciting. The company covered all the moving expenses; along with transporting my horse, Jasper. I needed to leave him behind; in order to get acclimated with the new surroundings, and finding a place to board. He was my baby, since I had owned him when he was a colt. The grandparents on my paternal side adopted a couple wild horses; they bred the female, and along came the cutest foal, Jasper. From the time I can recall, I was always infatuated with horses. As a youngster, I wanted to be a girl farmer with a horse. I was at the age of twenty when he arrived; my grandparents knew how desperately I wanted one. However, they wouldn't just release him to me without proving to them first that I was capable in handling the responsibility. After a year of demonstrating that I was committed and responsible, I was able to relocate him to a boarding facility closer to home. However, I had made arrangements with my family, to take care of him during this transition.

In the middle of summer of 1992, we relocated into a two-story apartment in Delaware, Ohio. Although, we arrived a day before the moving company delivered our possessions, so we had to sleep on the hard floors. We weren't completely alone in the strange area; other employees and their families also relocated into the same vicinity. We were only there for a month or so, and becoming acclimated with our new surroundings, when Daniel received instructions that the company was relocating us again, this time it would be Muskegon, Michigan. With all the consolidation, from the sale of the companies, they were closing the Ohio's location. This time, my husband, along with the other employees, relocated without us wives, in order to find a place to reside. I spent a month on my own, in a strange area; while Daniel was being entertained in Michigan, with his coworkers. I was not thrilled, with this arrangement. I was lonely, bored, and didn't know what to expect, when I would eventually relocate. He would call and elaborate regarding our new surroundings, but it was difficult to visualize without experiencing it, first hand.

Feeling Stability

Everything happened as expected, from finding an apartment, and organizing the moving company; to arrive as the same day we sign the lease. As soon as, they picked up our possessions in Ohio, I drove to Michigan. I drove five hours, but this time with no excitement or expectations, for I didn't feel secure enough about a long-term future in this location. The very first night, we decided not to unpack; instead, we decided to drive out to Lake Michigan which was only fifteen minutes from where we were living. In the summertime, the community puts up two large enclosed tents, with a wide variety of beer to choose from, and live music. The men, had already experienced this before, while getting acclimated with the area, and said, they enjoyed it. They were definitely correct! It changed my attitude about relocating here, and my outlook turned brighter. The community was sociable, and the atmosphere seemed exuberant. Three months, and no further instructions on transferring to another location; so, I felt secure enough to transport Jasper. I found a gorgeous boarding facility with acres of land to ride; at a cost, which was reasonable and included clean stalls. It was definitely an upgrade from where he's located in PA, which made me content. Jaspers entire travel, consisted of two days with an over-night, after crossing the border in Ohio, due to the number of hours allowed in the horse trailer. I discovered he was traveling with one of Oprah Winfrey's horses; with this information, I knew he would arrive safely. The anticipation was overwhelming until he finally arrived, which was shown through my emotions; but I was afraid he wouldn't recognize me, since it had been approximately six months. They walked him off the trailer backwards; I dashed over and gripped the lead. When Jasper and I locked eyes, the bond between us was never broken, and my guilt from leaving him behind diminished. My baby was back, which made my heart full again, and it began to feel like home.

 Over the course of time getting acquainted with the area, my insecurities diminished, and I started looking for employment. While looking through the newspaper ads, I found a Travel Consultant position available in a small quaint town, right on the lake called Grand Haven, it was only half hour away from home. I arrived at the Travel Agency, handed the manager my resume, and immediately, she interviewed and hired me on the spot. I started working the following day.

With both of us being employed, we opened a mutual savings account, and by the summer of 1993, we purchased our first home. The home was under construction; but only had minor details to finish before moving in. It was a single-family home that consisted of three bedrooms and one full bathroom. It was located at a dead-end street; nice for privacy and sitting on a 1/2 parcel wooded sized lot. The dark-brown wooded siding, blended in with all the beautiful trees surrounding the house. There were a pair of glass double doors off the living room, which opened onto a partially surrounding wooden deck, so you can observe the breathtaking scenery. It was the perfect home for first-time buyers, and we're delighted to purchase and choose the interior designs.

Now a bit settled in, I had this urge to proceed college. I didn't have a major in mind, but I followed my gut, and went to night school, at Muskegon Community College. I took a couple courses at a time and was academically motivated because I enjoyed being a student, plus the professors were amazing.

During my ritual of working full time, going to college, and enjoying my new life in Michigan, we needed to drive to Pennsylvania for a celebration. My mom married on June 28, 1993. Maybe, the fourth times a charm? They held a small ceremony outside their home, which included his three sons and Mom's three daughters. In the end, we must have looked like the Brady Bunch.

One day, while working, a woman strolls into the office. I questioned, if I could offer assistance with travel arrangement, and her response was no, but I would like to hire you. My jaw must have dropped to the floor, because she's a complete stranger and I'm fairly new in town. I was thinking to myself; this woman is bold, coming into the office trying to snatch their employees. I wasn't satisfied at this agency, because my boss never committed to her hours, while I worked excessively due to her lack or work and not being compensated for the extra time. I sat at my desk, listened intently, and answered all her questions. The lady owned a Travel Agency along Lake Michigan in Grand Haven, and guaranteed a phenomenal pay raise. My name had circled around town from previous clientele I had assisted with booking their travel arrangements. Walking out the front door, she handed me her business card, advised me to ponder, and give her an answer by the following week. It would have been foolish not to take the job. After pondering for a while, I decided to accept her offer. Switching employment was the best decision I ever made. I absolutely adored the owner and the part-time agent that worked periodically. The location was amazing; because during lunch hour, I would stroll the boardwalk, along the lake, and enjoy my meal. As an animal lover, we already had adopted two cats. I talked Daniel into getting a puppy. Golden Retrievers were attracting my attention; so, I started looking in the newspaper ads, and found five Golden Retriever puppies for sale. The ad declared two females and three males. I called the phone number right away and all the puppies were sold except one. Without hesitation, I told the gentleman that it's mine. I had worked the previous day, and we made arrangements for the gentleman to deliver the puppy to the agency, which Daniel would come and transport him home. When he arrived, the puppy was in a little box; desperately trying to get out. Without any expectations on the appearance of the puppy, he turned out to be the cutest, red-colored golden I have ever seen. (Red Goldens, are not as common as the cream-colored ones; therefore, it was a nice surprise.)

Once Dreyfus was trained (which took longer than usual, since we're first-time dog owners), we talked about starting a family.

Our First Born

I was still appearing in night courses, working full time, and in my mind getting pregnant could take time, so, I was patient when we started trying, without contraceptives. It didn't seem as though we were rushing the situation, but tried hard enough where the sex became less enjoyable, and more like a chore, but became pregnant instantly. During the nine months of pregnancy, everything went smoothly except, I was exhausted constantly, and decided to end my college career. Working full time and courses at night, was a nightmare; concentration and retaining material became non-existent. Besides exhaustion, no morning sickness or cravings, but gained thirty-eight pounds, from retaining fluids. Due to the swelling, the jewelers had to remove my wedding ring with pliers. We decided against, acquiring the sex of the baby; since we wanted to be surprised. Everyone was predicting a boy, since I was carrying low; my belly was practically upon my lap. Feeling the movement for the first time; is when all the excitement and amazement started to surface, as this little bundle of joy was growing inside. Occasionally, you could see the outline of the foot, when it was kicking or stretching.

It was in the middle of the night, and my water broke. I decided to take a shower before continuing on our way to the hospital. After arriving, they wheeled me into a private room for delivery. The nurses connected me to the monitors for the baby and myself. (I absolutely disliked the screen that displayed the contractions approaching). I tried breathing as they taught me in Lamaze classes; but found it unhelpful. I had to continue into my own trance, in order to move through each contraction. At one point the baby was pushing on my spine; which was so painful, it made me vomit (or, maybe it was the smell of Daniel's breakfast, while I was in excruciating pain). My family was continuously calling, and my boss was sitting outside the room anxiously awaiting, for the arrival; hearing her voice, did she have it yet? It definitely wasn't a calm environment while having this baby. The doctor declined the epidural, stating I was progressing quickly. I think the doctor was insane, because fourteen hours later; on May 27, 1994, I delivered a healthy seven pounds two ounces, baby girl and we named her Aubrey. All the pain, throwing up, and defecating on the table, during delivery; was all worth the experience. After the nurses placed her in my arms; she looked up at me with those gray blue eyes, and black hair sticking straight out everywhere, like static electricity; only then, I felt the beauty, of unconditional love. When we brought her home, I attempted to breast feed, but my breast milk production never came about. The doctors informed us to switch to formula since she was losing too much weight. Soon after she started drinking formula, another issue arose; she became colicky. Every night, from four to eleven p.m., she would scream at the top of her lungs and cry non-stop. Daniel and I would take turns, even when he was working; trying to soothe her pain. We tried everything to help the agony, with no success, and we became exhausted. The doctor suggested a certain brand of formula for sensitive stomachs; which I switched to, but still had the same issue. We couldn't go out in public places because you never knew when she would have a flare up. It was impossible to enjoy her as a newborn because it went on for months.

Not long after Aubrey was born, Daniel's company wanted to relocate us again, this time it was Texas. I thought to myself, let's give this a chance; I've become adventurous because of the last two moves. His immediate response was; hell no, I hate the cowboys! With that being said, we decided to move back to Pennsylvania. He found a position available with Bell Atlantic. Since he was an excellent candidate for the position, they hired him, almost immediately.

The entire process fell into place while relocating back to Pennsylvania. Our house sold within a month, the new employment was flexible on his starting date, found a boarding facility for Jasper, and I was able to use the same company to transport him back. With the transformation occurring quickly, and we didn't want to spontaneously buy another home; my mom and step dad had suggested residing with them, until we find a proper home. We gratefully, accepted their offer. My parents arrived a couple days before closing was scheduled for the house to assist with Aubrey and packing up our belongings. We were only in the house for a year; but with the total number of boxes, we filled; it seemed as if we were there forever. I didn't realize how exhausting relocating could be, because the last two moves; his company hired a moving company, and they handled everything. The day of closing on the house, Mom headed back to Pennsylvania with Aubrey while Daniel and my step dad picked up the moving van. Once they returned, we had immediately started loading the boxes. The only break we took was the hour at closing during mid-afternoon. I didn't feel attached to the house which made signing the papers effortless, and ready for the next phase in life. The new owners allowed us to spend the night; since we weren't finished packing and it was a long drive home to Pennsylvania. It was approximately nine p.m. when the house was completely vacant, but a couple of blankets to lay upon while we slept on the floor. We initially planned on getting a good night rest before heading home, but as all three of us laid there wide awake; and in unison, we said, let's go! My step dad and Daniel alternated with driving the U haul, while I followed behind with the car. Our ten-hour drive became more like thirteen hours, with all the pit stops for coffee and bathroom breaks; in order to stay awake. The next morning, when we arrived home; our belongings, except the necessities for Aubrey and pieces of clothing, were put into a storage unit until we find our own house.

    Daniel started working immediately after our return while I stayed home with Aubrey. I was intending on getting back into the work force, but not until we figured out the location of our new home. In the meantime, Mom was still working the night shift; which meant I had to keep Aubrey quiet during the day, while she slept. Unfortunately, she was still colicky, and I was unsure when she'd start screaming and crying. I spent every day outside walking her around in the stroller. Most weeks consisted of researching homes; and ultimately it paid off. We had found a three-bedroom, two and ½ bathroom, modern style looking home with vaulted ceilings that was under construction in a decent size neighborhood. It had a stone front faced with many shades of brown colors, and the rest of the home had tan siding. It had quite a few windows, and sliding glass doors which each led onto wooden decks; all perfect to allow the sunshine through. The house was built on a steep hill, which eventually flattened out as you came around the one-car garage. A small stream and forests divided the property line. After our walk through, we instantly thought this is ideal for our family; another great starter home, that fell into our laps. The location was a little more in the countryside than I liked, but the house and school district made the final decision. Our offer was accepted, and we relocated by the end of summer of 1994.

After relocating and getting acclimated once again, with our new life; I started looking for employment; and searching for a daycare, I could trust. Eventually, I was hired for a management position at a travel agency; which also required periodically, to observe and organize meetings with two other agency's that were nearby. All three agencies, were connected; but didn't have management until I was hired. I found an in-house daycare, toward work and near the house just in case there was an emergency. It absolutely broke my heart leaving Aubrey at daycare, but enjoyed working. Aubrey was five months old when I returned to work, and at this age, she was able to scoot around in her walker. I worked Monday thru Friday, from eight a.m. to five p.m. Before they hired me, the travel agency went through a huge turnover, with a new owner, and they lost most of their clientele due to the travel agents quitting. I hired a friend of mine that I worked with previously, hoping she would bring in business from her clientele. (Working in this business, you create a bond with the clientele, and they will stay loyal). Travel Agencies, earned commission from the airlines and tour operators. The more you booked, the higher the commission rate the agency would receive. But six months later on, the agency was still under turmoil from all the changes and wasn't producing enough to profit. My "friend," took it upon herself to advise the owner; it was my work ethic that isn't bringing in business. All agents among the three locations disagreed with what the owner had been advised. I believe my "friend" would have liked my position and attempted to sabotage me. The owner brought the issue to my attention, and wanted me to work longer hours. My reply, was hell no, I have a baby at home. I handed in my resignation, and never looked back. With freedom not working every day, I walked around the neighborhood and became friends with a few of the women. We were all around the same age, and so were our babies. Playdates were put on my calendar, until I received an unexpected phone call. The travel agency that I was employed at before marriage tracked me down and invited me back. They were notified from a mutual friend that I moved home. Instantly, they offered me a position and advised that the previous manager had been let go. As soon as we came to an agreement with the salary, I accepted. I found Aubrey a daycare center right behind the office building, and fortunately, had an opening for her age group.

It felt amazing being back at the agency. It had always been a small office that consisted of two-three salary agents, and some outside agents who operated strictly on commission, with no set hours. Previously, I left all my old clientele behind when I got married and relocated because I wasn't sure when I would be employed during the transition. After my return, most of the familiar clients were still booking their travel arrangements there, and were ecstatic to hear my voice.

Second Born

Our family life became pretty simple without having to relocate constantly; we were finally, able to feel some stability within our lives. Feeling secure made me a social butterfly within our new neighborhood. I made some friends during the time in between employment, and now since we lived there longer than usual, I practically knew the entire neighborhood. Since most of the adults were around the same age, and so were our children; there would be parties almost every weekend, that we would attend. Sometimes, on a Friday night after work, we would all wander around with a cold brew and never get back home until late at night. I came to realize, that living in the neighborhood, brought to the surface, what had been hiding within, all this time which was me. I was a very responsible Mom, and I liked to have fun too. My inner child was coming out to play. As I was spreading my wings, I noticed my husband wasn't as social. During gatherings, he would depart, and go home to watch TV or go to bed, while I stayed behind and socialized. I don't know why; but I always felt remorseful, even though I pleaded for him to stay (which was useless, since he already made up his mind). It was nice at times, since he would take Aubrey home and put her to bed; but I also wanted to enjoy the evening with him too. We never argued or raised our voice to one another; we just accepted what it is.

As Aubrey was getting older, and easier to manage; therefore, I had the urge to travel again. I would come across these amazing rates for travel agents, which would be foolish not to take the opportunity (three nights with airfare and hotel to Rome, Italy for $350.00). First, I asked Daniel to join me, but he was unable, due to work related issues; so, I asked a friend across the hall. We packed our suitcases and went to Italy for a long weekend; which included a train ride to Florence for the day. Not long after the last trip, I went to London for a long weekend, with a group of friends and took a tour to Stonehenge. Daniel didn't mind, as he was content staying home working and watching Aubrey. By this time, she wasn't a baby, but a toddler. I was enjoying life with traveling, working, being Mom, and a loving husband that lets me be who I am. Whatever we did as a family or couple; together or separate, it worked for us.

Aubrey was nearly two years old, when we decided to have another child. It didn't feel like a chore, this time around; and I became pregnant, almost instantly. The pregnancy went smooth, just like the first one; although, the one blood test the doctor ordered, came back high for possible down-syndrome. I went into the hospital, during lunch break, and had an amniocentesis procedure done. A week later, I received a phone call at the office, confirming everything was normal, and then they asked if I wanted to know the sex of the baby. Daniel and I had already agreed that we wanted to acquire the sex of the baby and the nurse informed me, we were having another girl. Neither of us cared about the sex, as long as it was healthy. I called Daniel immediately, after I hung up, and advised him the good news; he was elated. Both of us had a feeling it was another girl, because of the way I was carrying again, very low. I only gained twenty-eight pounds, even though I ate three meals a day. This pregnancy, my body didn't retain fluids which made a big difference. I exceeded my due date, so, the doctor placed Prepidil gel around the cervix, in hopes of inducing labor and a week later, I started having contractions.

My half-sister and nieces were over visiting when my contractions started; Daniel had just walked through the front door when I said, "I think it's time." All of us sat there and anxiously watched the clock ticking; sure enough, they were five minutes apart. I called my mom to meet us at the hospital because she was taking care of Aubrey, while the baby was born. Within the delivery room, I went to the bathroom to make sure I didn't defecate during giving birth again. The nurses hooked me up to all the monitors, and the contractions were still five minutes apart. The doctor finally arrived, to see the progression; this time, he had to break my water, which caused the contractions to become stronger and more frequent. I went into a trance, in order to deal with the pain, but as they were becoming intense, I broke down and asked the doctor for some relief. Unfortunately, the drugs they prescribed, relaxed me too late, because by this time, I felt the need to push too soon. After only being in labor for five hours (which was a lot shorter than the last one at fourteen hours); I had a seven pounds eight ounces, healthy baby girl on April 26, 1997, and we named her Kinsley. The pain medicine made me very loopy, to the point where I couldn't see straight and my hearing was impaired. It was like listening to Charlie Brown and the Peanut's schoolteacher. I don't remember the nurses placing her on my stomach, and Daniel cutting the cord. To make matters worse, when the doctor pulled out the placenta, it broke inside. The doctor rushed to remove every piece, I was bleeding profusely, and my blood pressure dropped to a scary level. I almost died after giving birth, and I have no recollection of the aftermath. I was unable to hold Kinsley until I had my strength back. Eventually, when I proceeded to the bathroom and glanced into the mirror, I almost passed out, because every blood vessel in my face busted! I appeared as something out of a horror movie. It felt like forever, but a day later, I was able to hold my precious little one. I may not have been able to see her during recovery; but I definitely heard her screaming down in the nursery. She had a set of lungs and attitude exactly like me.

    Three days later, I was released from the hospital and completely regained my strength, along with the blood vessels on my face slowly disappearing. Daniel and I agreed that with such complications after the delivery, this would be our last child. I wasn't emotional about our decision, because I have acknowledged of not wanting children after thirty, and I was twenty-eight when giving birth. Having a second child, you would think it would be less difficult, since you knew what to expect, but not this baby; she was born with a mind of her own. Kinsley was also colicky, which the doctor said it could be hereditary. It wasn't as severe and didn't extend the amount of time, like Aubrey had. As Kinsley was going through intestinal issues, she also had a reflux which caused her to projectile after feeding time. I wore half of the formula she drank, and needed to change clothing throughout the day. Eventually, I had to schedule a doctor's appointment, because she wasn't gaining weight. That itself, was never enjoyable, as she had such a vendetta against doctors. As soon as they came into the room, and she recognized their white coat; all hell broke loose. Most of the time, the doctors and I had to carry out sign language, because of her high pitch screech the entire time. Whatever the doctor prescribed, helped with the reflux, but the colic lasted awhile longer.

Neither of our infants were enjoyable; in fact, it was the most stressful and heartbreaking time, as they were suffering throughout the duration of infancy. But experiencing motherhood is when I truly understood, what unconditional love was all about.

Family Lifestyle

First Vacation without Children

After Kinsley was born, I started working immediately, because the owner of the travel agency, allowed me to work from home, as an outside agent. Having to put an infant and toddler in daycare, would likely consume my entire paycheck. Now however, my work was based solely on commission. This transition was brand new to the company, but the manager did an amazing job, keeping track of the commission that would be payable directly to me. The change progressed smoothly and everyone was pleased with the transition. I enjoyed working from home, as I had freedom throughout the day, where I could take the girls on daily field trips or a stroll in the park. I never really liked sitting at a desk for eight hours (as my mom always said, I had ants in my pants!). It drove me insane, and the majority of the time; I'd walk around instead of sitting at my desk. The clientele I had, were very flexible with timeframe; if they left a message, I was never advised to promptly return their calls. They made my occupation worth it. I took a pay cut, but Daniel and I worked through the change.

Even though, I worked from home, I attended the one a month meeting with the Eastern Travel Association. This allowed me to be connected with all the tour operators, airlines, and cruises. The meetings were very informative on all the updates and changes that needed to be addressed. The best part involving certain meetings were the free prizes given away, and some were even trips. One night, I met some colleagues at the Eastern Travel Association tradeshow; and they pulled my name! I almost keeled over because I never won anything in my life, and it happened to be a free trip to Bermuda. It included a three-night stay at the Elbow Beach Resort & Spa, and airfare on American Airlines.

I was beaming the entire way home, and thought for sure Daniel would inform me to take a friend due to his excessive workload. The last trip the two of us took together was Germany when I was seven months pregnant with Aubrey. To my surprise, he accepted my invitation. I booked our mini-vacation over my birthday; which happened to be the same day Princess Diana passed away in the car accident on August 31, 1997. My mom babysat both girls; by this time, Aubrey was three years old and Kinsley was four months. We weren't traveling for a long period of time, and we trusted them in my mom's care, which she was an amazing grandma! The trip turned out reinvigorating, as we had quality time to get reacquainted with one another, since once you start a family, the focus is the children. The only disappointment, from the entire trip was not renting mopeds to get around the island, because Daniel thought it would be too dangerous. Instead, we rode the bus around; which didn't take you to the secluded areas where all the beauty from the pink sand beaches were untouched. Our personalities were different in that aspect; I was the adventurous one, never giving it a thought about the outcome, and Daniel was the conservative one. During the marriage, our personalities balanced one another.

<u>New Neighbor Bondage</u>

When we lived in our neighborhood for four years, I experienced an unexpected surprise. A family of five, moved into our development from Canada. The couple had three girls; one was Aubrey's age, and the other two were a year or two older. I met the family from mutual friends who lived across the street during a gathering they were hosting. While engaging in conversation with Elaine, there was an instant connection and so did our girls. She was a stay-at-home-mom, and I worked from home with flexibility; so, we started arranging plans together with our children. By the time the gathering ended, we became best friends. Every day, we gathered mostly at Elaine's home since it was more spacious than mine. The children played amazingly well together, and her oldest daughter would look after Kinsley since she was one, going on twenty. There would be at least an hour every day for arts and crafts because the children loved to create. It felt like we had our own daycare center with the five children! Whenever Daniel came home from work, he knew where to locate me. Elaine and I would make cocktails and dinner for everyone; including our mutual friends that lived across the street from me.

Elaine and I became inseparable to the point where, if Kinsley couldn't locate me inside the house, she would slide open the screen door, close it, and walk down to Elaine's house. Luckily, nothing happened while she was strolling down to her second family's home. I was living the dream, perfect job, family, neighborhood, and friends.

<u>*Natural Disasters and a Need to Relocate*</u>

There was one slight problem where we resided, our finished basement would flood every time we had torrential downpour.

After all the aggravation and distress, when it will occur again, we decided to relocate. We researched housing approximately around the same vicinity, where we previously lived before marriage. The towns around that area were ranked in the top ten for being one of the best school districts. Knowing the statistics, made our decision easier, for where we wanted our permanent residence. A good education was one of our top priorities for the girls. It was exhausting reviewing all housing options that were available; they were either out of our price range or weren't up to our standards. Finally, one day after months of researching, we came upon a piece of land for sale. It never crossed our minds to build a home, until that day. The disadvantage was the location, because it wasn't within a development like we're accustomed to. There was only a total of nine homes on that street. The rest of the area was farmland. It will be a big adjustment for myself and the girls as we were accustomed to a larger tight-knit neighborhood. After weighing out the differences and desiring to be a part of this community, we purchased the land. The process proceeded as we had planned; the land was paid off within a year. We found a builder, (which was an acquaintance that lived diagonally across the street from our home) and selected a house plan, which required an architect.

    The time had come to sell our home. First, we attempted for sale by owner; offering open houses during the weekends. There were prospects, but never offered a proposal. After a while, we started feeling that most individuals, searching for a home, might be skeptical for this kind of sale. We decided to hire a real estate agent. They arranged all the paperwork and accepted two percent commission. The house sold instantly! In the course of closing on our previous home, we broke ground in late spring of 1999, for our permanent residence. The new owners agreed to rent the house to us for a couple of months, in hopes the construction would be completed within the end of the summer and not be homeless.

Overcoming Obstacles

Building a home was one of the most stressful times we had ever endured during our marriage. The weather was not cooperating, which eventually, pushed everything behind. It turned out to be one of the wettest summers with even hurricanes that came through. We may have lived inland, but the torrential downpours lasted days, caused it to flood everywhere. All our packed boxes were in their basement, and sure enough; the basement flooded. We had to call the new owners in the middle of the night, to advise them of the disaster. Again, Daniel had a gut feeling, which was always right; and unfortunately, we lost almost everything.

Since the timeframe of moving into our new home was pushed behind, we made alternate plans. We had to depart our old house by October, Mom invited us to reside with them until the house was completed. September of 1999 came quickly and Aubrey started kindergarten. I contacted the elementary school in the new district, and showed documentation we were in the process of building. The township also scheduled a date for the final inspection in order for her to attend kindergarten. When she was approved, I drove forty-five minutes one way and stayed within the vicinity until school was finished for the day. Kinsley was not amused, so we spent majority of the time at the playground.

My clientele was very understanding and patient regarding the dilemma; therefor, they never released my services to a different travel agent. I usually, worked evenings, since Daniel was home from work and could attend to the girls while I was working.

It was October 1, when we relocated with my parents. We put all our possessions into a storage unit, except for my desk. The girls slept in their spare rooms while Daniel and I slept on a blow-up mattress in the basement. My parent's dog was not thrilled with constant commotion, as he would leave a nice present, only on my side of the mattress.

After we left our previous development, there was a sadness from the loss that I felt within. Instantly, I sensed a disconnect from Elaine and neighbors that I had left behind. It completely changed the dynamics, where I would stroll down the road, visit everyone, and wouldn't arrive home until evening; and now it was a forty-five- minute drive one way. Even though it felt different, I made certain to stay in touch and accept the changes that occurred.

Residing with my parents didn't seem as stressful as the previous time, since the girls were older and Mom worked the day shift. Just about every day, Daniel and I would drive to the house and examine what the builder had accomplished. Whenever the neighbors happened to be outside, they would come over and start conversation. Even though it was stressful building a home, watching the process and feeling the excitement, that soon there would be anticipation upon completion, made up for all the agony.

Finally, right before Christmas 1999, while waiting patiently with anticipation, we relocated in our gorgeous home. After visualizing the design on paper for months, and once it was built, it nearly took my breath away. The design we chose, turned out remarkable! It was a two-story, single family style home; two-car garage, four bedrooms, and two and half baths. The front was brick faced along with maroon shutters, and tan siding. As soon as you walked through the front door, you automatically saw the climb of the cathedral ceiling, which led into the living room. There were plenty of windows in each room, and sliding glass doors that opened up onto a wooden deck. The views from the windows toward the rear of the home, was picturesque; because of the beautiful horses that had grazed, from a boarding facility that ran behind our property line. In the corner of the main living room, sat a cozy propane fireplace with a wooden mantel. The kitchen wrapped around the living room with a walk-in pantry and eat in bump out. Although, with the open floor plan we selected; eventually, turned into a school track field, as the children started running around. After moving in without final inspection, (apparently, the township doesn't follow protocol, since they never responded to our builder's messages) our family was able to enjoy Christmas and ring in the New Year with joy. The entire family started our normal routines; I worked from home, Daniel worked at his office, and Aubrey was in full time kindergarten.

Summertime came quickly, when I started socializing with the surrounding neighbors. The township also held summer camp for children; so immediately, I signed both girls up. I started conversing with the parents during drop off and pick up times for the children. I immediately bonded with one of the moms, named Carla, and through the course, we became best friends. Her daughter was a couple years older than Aubrey and her son, and Kinsley was the same age. As time passed, our friendship flourished and our families developed into one. Both families organized trips or gatherings; from camping, hiking, fishing, boating, to spending every holiday with one another. It was beautiful watching our families grow and blossom together; all the love and support between us, the bond will be embedded in my heart forever.

Difficult Losses

On April 22, 2003, I received a phone call advising me that Dad passed away. He was recently put in a nursing home, due to his instability as he was getting older, caused from the stroke. The home, he previously lived at, couldn't take care of him any longer since he became stubborn. He wouldn't listen or wait for assistance. Therefore, he would hurt himself while losing his balance. One incident, after collapsing, the doctor sewed staples in his head due to an enormous gash. I would visit occasionally, and sometimes the girls would accompany me. The love for my father faded away with our distant relationship, but I felt it necessary to stay in touch since he was my dad. On numerous occasions, I would question him with regarding the abuse we endured, and his only response was, "I'm sorry, I don't know." I never received a true confession on the sexual abuse toward me as he denied the allegations to my mom. The only way to move forward and release the trauma was to forgive him; and that's what I did at his funeral. Around the same year of my dad's death, I had to make one of the toughest decisions of my life; putting Jasper down. He was only thirteen at the time, when he was diagnosed with a genetic disorder; called Founder, also known as Laminitis. It's inflammation of the laminae of the foot, which the soft tissue structure that attaches the coffin or pedal bone of the foot to the hoof wall. The inflammation and damage to the laminae causes extreme pain and leads to instability of the coffin bone in the hoof. Even with all the medicine that was provided; he wasn't able to walk up to the gate for his meal. He was always such a pig when it came to eating, so I knew right then it was time to set him free, from all the pain. It was a cool rainy day, when the veterinary came and explained the process. I was sobbing uncontrollably, so Daniel had to take the lead while the veterinary injected the serum. Once he fell to the ground and pronounced dead, I laid there hugging his lifeless body; explaining how much he was loved and will be forever missed. The boarding facility covered him with a tarp, as it took two days for the company to retrieve his body.

Our family life became pretty hectic, as our girls were growing older. Both were in several sporting events, since we let them try out for any sport they wanted, until it became too competitive; then, they had to choose one. Aubrey became a soccer player and Kinsley was a gymnast. The sporting life took most of our time traveling back and forth to practices, games, and competitions. Daniel and I would go in opposite directions; but for most part, when it came down to games and competitions, we were able watch them together. By this time, the girls were old enough to get themselves on the bus for school, so I took the manager position that was available in the office. I made sure I only worked until three p.m. since I needed to transport Kinsley to gymnastics practice. The practices consisted of six days a week with a three-hour session time and longer on Saturdays. I felt like I lived out of my vehicle, between work and running to practices. Most nights, I wouldn't get home until late evening. It turned out to be extremely lengthy days with juggling work and Kinsley's sport; but I wouldn't change a thing, as long as they were happy and putting in the effort.

Transformation

Energy Shifts

Through the years of becoming older, I've noticed a personality shift. I started becoming more of an entertainer and organized gatherings that made me thrive on pleasing others, and in return, made them happy. Hosting parties became my specialty; especially around the holidays. I also organized a Girls Cruise, which started during the month of October. It began as a three-day cruise with Carla, and another close friend, Leigh. We weren't sure if our husbands could handle the children while we're gone but they did an absolute remarkable job. Every year, we felt more comfortable leaving our children behind, so we added more days onto the cruise, and invited more women to join. After expressing how much I enjoyed my time; I tried convincing Daniel to join a man's trip, but he wasn't interested. He was never sociable and entertaining like me; but by no means disregarded my wants and needs. Since we had been married for quite some time, we molded into one another. True marriage is desiring both partners to be happy and that was our goal. Even with hosting gatherings, it took him several years to relax and enjoy the moments of laughter; only then my mission was accomplished, I finally saw him living in the moment.

Our relationship, through the years of marriage became stronger, even during the pressure from family life, and his career. I can honestly say, we had the perfect marriage. Fights were pretty much nonexistent; I can only recall, maybe two arguments, and didn't last for a long period of time. His demeanor was very tolerant and patient. For instance, whenever I sent him to the grocery store, and he would return with the wrong item, or not the sale priced item that I requested, I would get mad; but he wouldn't say a word and walk away. Sometimes he was to patient, especially when it came down to disciplining the girls. That part about his personality didn't resonate well with me because he didn't like confrontation. It caused me to be the mean Mom, since I was the disciplinarian. I needed more support in that area which I had asked for numerous times. There was a moment in my life, where Kinsley forced me into a depression, because of her attitude during puberty. We argued constantly, and Daniel wouldn't have my back. Eventually, after impelling him out of his comfort zone, he would take the girls in a separate room and have a conversation, about their behavior. Whenever he talked, they would listen, as it was very rare of him to intervene. We were very honest and open with one another. So, the trust in our relationship was never shattered. Our love for one another allowed us to accept the differences, but also pushed each other in order to grow.

March of 2010, I was approved for my own in-home travel agency, which I named, Sandy Beach Travel. The previous agency I worked for, closed their doors due to lack of funds. The internet was taking over, and pushing the smaller agencies out of business. I always loved working from home, because it gave me more freedom, as I never liked sitting at a desk for hours answering phone calls. A couple years later, I added on a doggie daycare/boarding business. My agency wasn't bringing in the profit that I was expecting, as I had to release most of my biggest corporate accounts to other agents through the transition. The internet was beginning to interfere with leisure travel, concerning packages. Booking packages is where you generate the most commission. Carla suggested, I should start a dog boarding business. I already did this, for another friend of mine when they vacationed. Most people dislike putting dogs in a kennel and instantly, it became a success! Sometimes, I would be walking ten dogs at a time, and people driving by would stop to take pictures. I received compliments constantly on how well behaved the dogs were and in synced with one another while walking. They were also astonished on how I controlled all of them at once. It just came natural to me; handling dogs and juggling the leashes, was one of my many surprised talents.

The Passing of a Best Friend

The year of 2012, was a very emotional year for me. First, I lost a dear friend of mine, Natalie to Leukemia. We had been best friends since high school, but then lost touch with each other over the years, due to her drug use. When she finally became clean and sober, is when the doctors informed her of the cancer. Immediately, we rekindled our friendship, and I helped her until the end. Unfortunately, the day she passed on; I was traveling with Aubrey on a celebratory cruise for her high school graduation. Even though I wasn't present during her final moment, I was in contact with my mom and had her rush to the hospital to put the cell phone up to her ear. As I was sobbing, I told her how the love of our friendship will never die; I would take care of her dog Romeo; and to send me a penny from heaven to let me know she's around. At that moment she was in a coma, but heard every word I said, because I found pennies everywhere throughout the cruise, and they still show up periodically to this day.

First Born Leaving the Nest

By fall, is when the second part to this emotional year began, because we were sending Aubrey to college, Indiana University of Pennsylvania. Eighteen years our lives revolved around our precious daughter and keeping her safe. Daniel and I were very emotional during our entire drive home. Leaving her at college, felt like a piece of me, left my soul. I knew deep within my soul this would be the best experience in her life, but broke my heart as she left the nest. I pulled in the faith that she would stay safe away from home. What pushed me through the heartache; was Kinsley at home, keeping me entertained. We had three more years until we were completely empty nesters, so all my energy and time was directed toward Kinsley. She was competing in gymnastics after taking a year off due to mental issues, and also became a pole-vaulter in high school track.

Road Trips with Our New Camper

During the final three years before Kinsley graduated from high school, our family was extremely busy which made the years pass by quickly. Daniel started traveling for his employment, and I was swamped with the dog business. During the spring, I would be dodging both sporting events, track and gymnastics meets, as I disliked missing any of them. We had bought a nice size camper that slept eight, that included a small bathroom, so we could eventually travel cross-country. My parents had given us their pop-up camper that we used for years, but disliked using public restrooms, so we sold it in order to upgrade. Our entire family, including the dog, loved camping, and we would allow the girls to take a friend along. Most of the time, my mother-in-law joined us too. At one point, we must have looked like the Griswold's, in the movie National Lampoons Vacation. The Chevy trailblazer would be packed to the max, as you could barely see the dog in the back. Each camping trip gave us fun filled memories that will last a lifetime; we still laugh at some of the stories. One trip, Kinsley gave herself a concussion by not paying attention to where she was going; instead, she was looking at her reflection in a store window and ran into a thick steel light post. Her hard head literally caused the post to sway. By early evening, Daniel and me drove her to the emergency room, since the goose egg on her head kept getting larger, and she felt nauseous. After countless hours in the hospital, it turned out, she had a concussion. We also took family vacations, from Disney World to cruises; but I think camping was our real way to relax, enjoy nature and be in the present moment. Sitting around campfires, making s'mores, and telling stories was our time of togetherness.

Empty Nesters

Every year I'd be asking myself, where does the time go? It felt like yesterday that I gave birth to these beautiful girls and now, I'm sending both to college. The same mixed emotions that I had felt before, came back around as I prepared to send Kinsley. Visiting colleges really puts it in perspective, I had never experienced visiting before, since Daniel explored them with Aubrey. I thought my emotions were bad before, but now, we're going to be empty nesters! My head was spinning while the heart ached. Eighteen years, all my time, energy, heart, and soul went into the girls I forgot who I truly was, other than a mom. I would be driving down the road and then all of a sudden, I would burst into tears thinking of the house being empty. Deep within, I was a lost soul. Kinsley and I visited four different colleges, and the fourth one was the charm. After filling out the application and writing her essay, she was accepted at West Chester University. Kinsley's senior year in high school flew by and so did the summer. Our truck was packed to the max again, and drove her to West Chester, on August, 2015. We arrived and helped set up her dorm, ate lunch, and explored campus. When we came to a halt, she turned around and said, "Mom, don't worry about me, I'll be fine." The tears swelled up as we hugged goodbye, then she walked away to explore her new home and make new friends. I don't think I had any more tears left to cry, since I had been emotional all year long, or maybe I came to peace with letting go. I didn't break down sobbing during the drive home, like I did previously, as we dropped off Aubrey at college the first year. It was eerily quiet around the house, but it didn't take long getting used to the empty nest syndrome; I was busy with the dog business and booking camping trips for Daniel and I. We always talked about taking the camper further south, so I started researching and booked a couple weeks in two different states.

Daniel still traveled at least one or twice a month on business, but the house and dogs kept me busy in his absence. Leigh, Carla, and I would attend happy hour once a week to keep acquainted. In the recent years, my annual cruises dwindled down to just Leigh and I. We decided to extend our cruises to eight-days. On October 2015, we booked a Halloween cruise on the Carnival Breeze. It was an eight-day Southern Caribbean cruise. Out of the entire fifteen girls cruises I had been on; this particular one, transformed my life forever.

Spiritual Awakening

Psychic Reading

I was living this amazing life with a perfect family. I had a beautiful home, friends, financially stable, and traveled around the world. But one day, I was blindsided; which ended up turning my whole world upside down.

A week before, our girl's cruise with Leigh, I decided to visit to a friend of mine who's a psychic. I had readings periodically, and held psychic parties at my home. She was usually accurate, and certain events came true. I believe in psychics, as I had unexplained experiences that had happened to me. For instance, I've had several outer body experiences while sleeping. One experience, I will never forget, is when I floated out of my physical body and into the bathroom to be greeted by my deceased horse. He wanted to show me that he's free of pain and can run again. I kissed his nose, hugged him around the neck; then he turned around and galloped away. Another outer body experience that will forever be embedded in my memory, was one night when I was visiting my deceased girlfriend. Our encounter wasn't long after she passed away.

Natalie was over the moon about my visit and wanted to show off her brand-new home. It felt so surreal, like she had never left the physical world as we were walking through her home, and she was complaining about the wooden deck not being constructed properly. After the tour, we climbed into her car, and she picked up the cell phone to call her boyfriend, that was still living. I glanced toward her and said, "How would he feel talking to a ghost?" We both started laughing hysterically, and that was the end of our visit. Having these experiences gave me peace and comfort, knowing that our loved ones and animals are still with us, even though they passed onto the other side.

When I walked into the psychic's office for a reading, the first thing that came out of her mouth was, "Who do you know that starts with the letter J? Because he'll be interfering with your marriage." After the reading, I left her office feeling perplexed, since the only "J" names that came to mind were married to my girlfriends, and there was no connection between us, other than a friendship. I pushed the reading out of my mind; thinking, maybe she had an off day and besides, I would never want to sabotage my marriage.

October 24, 2015, Leigh and I checked in for our cruise and went straight to the lido deck to buy a drink. The first day we arrived on the ship the weather was perfect, sunny and warm. Both of us love to soak up plenty of sun, before heading back north where it's cold and snowy. We picked out our spot by the outdoor swimming pool, laid our towels on the lounge chairs, consumed our drinks, and then proceeded to the dining area for lunch. After doing this for fifteen years, we had our routine down pat. By five o'clock, the horn blew, and we set sail. The only thing we disliked about cruising was mandatory muster drills, as we were already tipsy by that time and chatted the entire drill. You're packed like sardines in a can, all formed in a row, at your assigned station. Once everyone is accounted for, the personnel proceeds with the instructions regarding how to exit in an emergency. After the drill, we walked back to the pool, and watched the ship leave Miami, while the entertainer director had music blaring and people dancing around the pool. Everyone was celebrating while departing for their vacation. I specifically made our dining reservations for eight-fifteen p.m. as it gave us more time to lounge in the sun, and didn't want to feel rushed at our ports of call.

Our set sail was absolutely amazing as we're both relaxed and living in the moment. After getting ready for the evening, we had extra time to stroll around the ship before heading to our assigned dining room for dinner. (We used to get lost and become directionally challenged, to the point where the key wouldn't unlock our cabin door. After entering the key multiple times, we finally realized that were on the wrong floor and on the other end of the ship; Alcohol might have had something to do with that. But now, we have become experts and never get lost). As we're walking around, we heard all this commotion coming from a place called, The Red Frog Pub. This was a fairly new ship, and the only one at the time, that offered this pub, so we walked in to see what all the commotion was about. It was so jammed packed with people that you could barely walk around without being pushed and shoved, but we did it anyway. Pushing our way through the crowd, we came upon a group of individuals gathered around a high-top table. They were laughing hysterically; I believe the captain could have heard them from the bridge. They stopped us in our tracks, and asked if we just witnessed what happened. We shrugged our shoulders and shook our heads no, and informed them we just arrived.

The Stranger

As we were having conversation with our new friends, a man came up from behind me and questioned, "What just happened?"

He was handsome, young, tall, and muscular, with black hair. He was definitely my type, if I was single and younger. I informed him that we had no clue what recently occurred, since we just strolled into the pub and didn't notice anything out of the ordinary. After all the chaos of whatever just occurred, we strolled out of the pub, informing our new friends that we will return after dinner. Throughout the ten-course meal, we were still giggling at what occurred in the pub, and the stranger that came from behind, that startled me. Leigh then informed me, that he was the musician, singing in the pub.

Obviously, I missed that completely, since I was trying to maneuver around the crowd. Both of us said in unison, "That's going to be our hangout for the week!" After eating our delicious meal and joking around with the waiters, we had rushed back to the Red Frog pub. We found out my stranger's name, which was Jackson; he was singing, and our friends were sitting at the same table. By this time, it was ten-thirty p.m., and it wasn't crowded like it was earlier. Our group was getting larger, as we gathered around the table and ordered drinks. I wasn't in the pub more than ten minutes, when Jackson arrived at our table and started a conversation with me. Eventually, he sat down with our group, during his breaks, and have conversation amongst everyone. By one a.m., the bar was winding down and most of our group departed, except Leigh and I. We stayed behind to interact with the pub staff and Jackson. At one point during the evening, Jackson and I would be sitting side by side, engaged in conversation, while Leigh was throwing nerf ball behind the bar with the staff. It felt oddly comfortable sitting alongside Jackson, in which, we had become close enough where our torsos would be touching; like I have known him forever, but he was a stranger, I just encountered. Leigh and I closed the bar, but stayed afterwards conversing with Jackson, until the staff finally kicked us out. With the astounding night and maybe a little intoxicated, we had cackled the entire way to the cabin. While getting ready for bed and talking about all the events that occurred throughout the evening; out of nowhere, I blurted out, I know Jackson, but not from this lifetime. That night, I fell asleep wondering about Jackson and our past life together, and if he was the particular one the psychic informed me about, since his name started with a 'J.' Throughout the cruise, Jackson and I would always run into each other; whether he was performing, or walking around at one of the seaports. Leigh and I became close friends with the pub staff; so, we would drop by before dinner to have a glass of wine and engage in conversations. Every time we were sitting there, Jackson would appear, say hello and hug me before proceeding away from the pub. With every interaction Jackson and I encountered, it became extremely intense to the point, where Leigh said, "It felt uncomfortable to be around us." The uncomfortableness had nothing to do with public affection since we never kissed; it was a sense of belonging. Whenever we were at the same location, he would stand by my side or shout my name while singing. The connection I experienced in each other's presence, felt like no other individuals existed in the room. My head would be spinning, as if I was in the middle of a wind tunnel, drawing me inward.

 During the entire cruise, I would try and detach myself from the experience I was enduring, since I was still married but apparently, my heart and soul knew otherwise. One of our seaports was Aruba, and Leigh and I decided to take the pub-crawl tour. It was evening, when we came upon one of the last pubs we visited. It was a beautiful night with the galaxy shining bright. At one point, I strolled outside and gazed at the twinkling stars and thought to myself, *I didn't feel the need to be married any more.* It was a calm and surreal moment of thought, but on the bus ride back to the cruise, questions started swirling around inside my head. I never discussed or required a divorce; but now, I felt this bizarre but amazing connection with Jackson. That night, as I was getting changed for dinner, I put on jewelry; except for my wedding ring. I left it in the safe, for the duration of the cruise. The cruise, was coming to an end, and my heart and soul felt very heavy. I didn't want to say goodbye to all our friends and most of all, Jackson. All the cruises we traveled on seemed to go by so quickly, but this particular one went like a snap of a finger, as we came upon our last night, which was Halloween.

Most of the people were dressed up in their costumes parading around the ship for the contest. Leigh and I stepped into the pub for a cocktail, and to watch some of the costumes going past, before heading to dinner for the last night. When we gathered around the table with our friends that were already present, Jackson came right over and gave me a hug. He was dressed like superman, and all I could remember was standing there dazed with sadness while rubbing his cape. Again, everyone was not existent but superman and I; but now, experiencing all these emotions that felt deeper than I have ever felt before, it drained the energy directly from my soul. After our cocktail, we advised everyone we'll be back and rushed off to dinner. I never ate so quickly in my life, but both of us desired to get back to the Red Frog pub for our last night. The dining room staff was absolutely amazing, so we gave them with a hug and waved them goodbye. Our friends were still gathered around the same table while Jackson was singing his favorite tunes. He had an amazing voice, and I could listen to it all night long. When his shift ended, everyone walked over to him, and said their goodbyes, while he provided them with business cards. Once people started leaving the pub, I slowly strolled over, and gave him a never-ending hug, and expressed how much I was going to miss him. During our embrace, some of our group decided to go next door to the dance club, and asked Jackson to join them. He agreed, but after he changed out of his costume. He strolled in the nightclub for no more than ten minutes, before leaving. As he was proceeding out of the club, I was standing near the dance floor. He came over and bumped me from behind, and when I turned around, he informed me that he was leaving. I questioned him as to why, but his only response was he needed to get up early. I looked perplexed, since he just changed out of his costume to celebrate one last time; but he gave me another hug goodbye. This time, it felt so surreal, as if we ended our relationship. My heart ached as he strolled out the door.

During the plane flight home, I kept asking myself, "What the hell just happened?" Luckily, Daniel was out of town on a business trip when I arrived home, so I could be alone and ponder over what transpired. After bringing in the suitcases from the truck, I immediately got on the computer, and sent Jackson an email advising him I had arrived back safely and missing his nightly hugs.

His only response was, "Glad you made it home safely, and this was one of the best cruises he experienced in a long time." I had a week to myself, which probably wasn't good because all I could think about was Jackson. The more I thought about him, the more confused and saddened I became. I kept asking myself, how could I have such strong feelings for someone I just met? We didn't even kiss or have any kind of affection other than hugs. There weren't even phone numbers exchanged between us. All I had was his business card with his email written on it.

Twin Flame

I have heard and experienced soul mates before; since I was married to one; but this was a totally different feeling of tugging and pulling me inward. So, I started researching on the computer about different soul mates and came across something called Twin Flame "soul mates." It stated that before coming to earth you share one soul; then you split into two in order to experience two different lives here in the physical world. They are a mirror image of yourself. I never heard of such a phenomenon; but the more I researched Twin Flames, I was adamant Jackson was mine. The sense of attraction, recognition and longing; not to mention the familiar feeling which causes an undeniably intense bond as though you have known them before. Bingo! It all made sense to me now. After coming to the conclusion, that Jackson was my Twin Flame; didn't make the situation any better; it actually made it worse. I was married and wouldn't even consider a divorce. I married for life, as I didn't want to become my parents and have children come from a dysfunctional family; even if they were grown.

Daniel came home from his business trip, and I felt totally distant and there was a sense of emptiness, knowing that I just met my other half. Being married for twenty years, he knew me inside and out. He would have caught on instantly with my body language that something wasn't right. We had a very honest relationship, so I could express anything without judgment; we thrived through it. Not knowing if he thought I was foolish or not, I proceeded to explain the entire story regarding Jackson on the cruise and him being my Twin Flame. During the explanation of what a Twin Flame represents, his face went completely blank as if he had seen a ghost or something, and the only words that came out of his mouth were, "What does that mean for us?" It took plenty of reassuring, to ease his mind that Jackson will never come between us; but at the same time, I was trying to convince myself as well. After weeks since the cruise, and being honest with Daniel, I tried to get back to some kind of emotional normalcy. The yearning for my other half never subsided, I just declined to let it ruin my family and accept the friendship that was formed. The last communication between Jackson and I was through email. I asked how he was doing, and he responded, "Great, I'm leaving the cruise industry after my contract ends and moving back home." Never giving it a second thought before I hit the send button. I expressed, to make sure he stops in Pennsylvania on his way home. No response, but a week later he invited me to be friends on Facebook and his music page, which I had accepted.

Searching for Clarity

The more I had dodged these feelings, the crazier I felt; because all I wanted was clarity. He never expressed any signs of emotions which confused the hell out of me. How could we be so different, emotionally? I went from psychic after psychic to help confirm whether he was my Twin Flame or not. After researching daily, in my mind he had to be, since everything I read, pertained to what I perceived. The feelings and emotions I felt were raw and heart breaking since he never reciprocated. I also researched that there were fake Twin Flames too, which had the same characteristics. It was all too confusing which made my head spin, but my heart was full of love for this man. Every psychic reading, I had experienced at this point, I ended up more confused than ever. They may have confirmed what I already suspected (that he's the one), but I was still at a loss because his actions weren't love, just friendship. Feeling like a puppet on a string, I was forced to accept what is. He was oblivious with our connection and I was married. Again, I went back to focus on Daniel and the family. Going through daily life, emotionless with my stomach all tied up in knots, and having to keep it hidden from the family, because someone else sucked the soul right out of me; this had become my new normal. I had witnessed via Face book that my Twin Flame started dating a woman that he met on a cruise, not long after mine. Gazing at pictures of the two of them, felt as though he ripped the heart right out of my chest and stomped on it. My soul literally went numb. I immediately stopped interacting with him on face book and didn't contact him through email. I believe their relationship only lasted a couple months or so; but once I knew for sure he was single again, I started feeling a sense of relief and was wandering if their breakup had anything to do with our connection.

 One night, Leigh and I met for happy hour. As soon as I sat down at the bar, I happened to look up and noticed a beer sign hanging on their wall. That particular beer was named and made in my Twin's hometown, Narragansett, Rhode Island. As the evening went on, I developed enough courage, with the support with Leigh, to take a picture of the sign and send it to Jackson through messenger, along with a message, asking if there was anything good that came from his town? This would definitely break the ice between the two of us. His contract had ended with the cruise industry, and he relocated home; his reply was almost immediately. That night, we rekindled our friendship.

 I was ecstatic we were friends again, but my heart and soul

ached for more. At this point, I felt like I was living a double life. My heart and soul belonged to Jackson, but on the other side, trying to live a normal life with a devoted husband and family. A week after my conversation with Jackson, Leigh and I were together again, and I sent him another message through messenger. This time when he responded, he provided me with his phone number. We texted back and forth throughout the evening. Daniel was on a business trip, so the house was empty. Just by texting him, I felt like I was having an outer body experience; and nothing existed but us. It was the exact same feeling I came across when we were together on the cruise. I went to bed with a smile on my face and heart racing like I had just ran a marathon. I woke up the next morning to a text from him, and it was a picture of an eggplant. Dumbfounded and confused on what this meant, I asked Leigh, and she had no idea either, but we had found out through her son. After researching sex emojis and their meanings, I sent one back. We joked back and forth and then all of a sudden, he quit texting. I instantly felt him pulling away. After pleading multiple times not to be silent he responded, "He's busy working." Following Jackson's absent interaction, I felt miserable after disregarding me, but had a little glimpse of hope that he was starting to feel the connection. Once in a while, I would send him a text asking how he was doing, or wishing him a happy birthday. He always responded but never into a full conversation. One night joking around, I sent him an emoji text referring to DNCE's song Cake by The Ocean. I thought it was creative and wanted to know what kind of reaction I would receive. I waited patiently for a response until the time passed and silence; which was abnormal, as he's usually quick to respond. I felt it in my gut that something was off, so I sent him another text advising him, there will be major changes heading my way. I didn't give it a second thought as to why or question the need to inform him of the information, as I hit the send button. Immediately this caught his attention and responded with an attitude and said, "And now you're telling me?"

I didn't care or want to know the reasoning behind his response, but all I said was, "Sorry, what do you want me to do?"

His final response was, "Nothing, I have to get back to work!" The connection between Twin Flames is usually chasing and running from one another. I now have been ghosted; which is typical between them.

I wasn't much of a chaser, per my personality; but I preferred to keep in touch periodically. Every time, I would send Jackson a text, I was still ghosted. As though it feels like a lifetime ago that I met Jackson; I have only been dealing with these, strong, intense, emotional roller coaster of a never-ending ride for almost a year. I was living a double life between Daniel, and now a soul relationship. I was not an actor with hiding my feelings, but Daniel never questioned the situation, and let me figure it out; in hopes, our marriage would get back to some kind of normalcy.

Psychic Abilities Formed

Ever since Jackson started rejecting me on the physical plane, our soul connection became stronger, along with psychic abilities that I never knew existed within me. I was already struggling with the soul connection, and now psychic abilities to the point where I thought, I was going insane, so Leigh advised me to meditate. I was always a busy body and never thought I had the power to go within, so she started me out with guided meditation. Eventually, I worked my way into silent meditation, which took a lot of discipline. By meditating, I was able to quiet the mind, which allowed me to accept the changes that were happening; because I had no other choice whether I wanted them or not.

The psychic abilities, that were being created, started from the way our two souls communicated through telepathy. First, it all began with interconnected thoughts. I would be outside walking the dogs, and then all of a sudden, I could hear his voice asking me a question, which then turned into a whole conversation. No wonder I thought I was going insane, talking to myself! Another day, again I was outside walking the dogs, I heard his voice singing a tune. I immediately, grabbed the cell phone from the pocket of my backpack; sure, enough he was singing that same tune, live on his music face book page. What a sigh of relief, I'm not crazy after all, since I had proof, to myself anyway. Although, this still didn't sway me one hundred percent, I wanted to try a little experiment. Whenever he planned on performing live on his face book page, he'll let the audience know which dates, by posting them. I picked a date when I was available, and watched him perform. I sent him a message telepathically on what song I wished to hear. Not soon after, he finished the song, he advised the audience, that he had no idea why he chose it, because it wasn't his style of music. Now, I had the confirmation.

My second psychic abilities that formed were visions, lucid dreams, and astral traveling which I had experienced one other time. They were always during the evening hours while I slept or close to dawn. The visions are like watching a movie strip or looking through a panoramic lens of a camera. The lucid dreams were when I was aware that I was dreaming, but was one of the characters in the dream and through astral traveling, I was able to leave my physical body and travel in the different astral planes. As I experienced each one of these, our two souls were connecting and pushing us forward to come home. I felt this unconditional love we had for one another; but when I woke, I was confused as hell because we weren't together in the physical world. I often pondered if he had the exact visions, dreams, and astral traveling that I experienced.

One of the very first lucid dreams I encountered, was watching a past life of the two of us playing hiding-go-seek with other kids. I asked a little girl what was my name, and she told me as they were running around trying to find a place to hide. I'm not sure what year it would have been, but it was very rural with dirt roads. The climate looked like summertime since the boys were wearing short outfits and the girls were in their little dresses. I'm guessing we were around five at the time. Jackson and I ended up hiding in the same shack when the vision jumped ahead with me standing in this amphitheater type building, being an adult and his mom standing beside me. There was a big white movie-screen showing videos and pictures of Jackson when he was a baby onto adulthood. Then all of a sudden, he appeared behind me. When we hugged, I immediately felt the unconditional love between us, and we were finally home. This one particular night as I was astral traveling, I was flying through mountains, and I was thinking to myself where am I going and why is it taking so long? Finally, I came upon an enormous house with balconies on each level. After I came to a halt, I happened to look up, and there was Jackson, standing on one of the balconies. I yelled his name with excitement, and when he came rushing toward me, I flew into his arms. Again, I felt like home.

The visions I had, started out slow, similar to watching one clip in a show or movie. For instance, one of my very first visions were having a picnic with Jackson. I could feel the love and comfort between the two of us, but then my vision ended.

Another experience was taking a shower together and engaging in sexual activity. I felt gloomy as I desired to watch more and feel the emotions of this clip, before awakening. After a while my visions became much longer, and one time with sound effects. The two of us were hiking up a mountain, until we came upon the peak. The scenery was picturesque as we gazed over the valley. Before heading down the mountain, we proceeded to snuggle and kiss until others started joining us. It felt like forever going down the mountain as it was steep and the wind started to blow. I could actually hear the swoosh during the vision, like I was physically present and feeling the hairs blowing into my face. As we proceeded down the mountain; at times, we had to step aside for others to pass, in order to move forward since the path was extremely narrow. This was only a fraction of visions and dreams I had experienced between us. The rest may perhaps be a book in itself.

All my psychic abilities that came to the surface occurred within the same timeframe. I had no choice whether I wanted them or not, so I just accepted my new way of life.

When the fourth psychic ability of emotions formed, it happened in the spring of 2016, as Daniel and I were traveling to California for Kinsley's gymnastics meet. While sitting on the airplane, I dosed off and had a quick vision of Jackson. Afterwards, I felt this weird sensation in my gut, like a cramp, but not painful. Even though it was a bizarre feeling, I brushed it off, thinking I devoured food that didn't agree with me. Then one night while sleeping in our hotel room, I woke up from a dream that I had of Jackson and felt a pull or tug in my gut. Now, I was feeling anxious because our souls were interacting with each other on numerous levels. I could feel his soul's emotions in my gut, whenever he wonders about me, and all the emotions that go along with our separation. Having a soul connection like this was very difficult, while lying next to Daniel in the bed and trying to focus on the marriage. Once in a while, I would go through a pissed off period; because our souls were forming a connection, but Jackson doesn't acknowledge that I exist. Then, there would be times during meditation, I could feel our souls pining for one another, and then sit there sobbing uncontrollably, placing my hands over my face; catching all the tears running down my cheeks. This occurred numerous times, and I went to bed emotionally exhausted. This part of a connection was very painful and confusing, but beautiful at the same time, since I could feel the pure unconditional love between our souls. The more I focused among our connection the stronger it became. Our souls started communicating telepathically to one another every morning; then, ultimately, we had sexual encounters. At that moment, I was in such disbelief and kept questioning myself, what the hell just happened? All these questions started swirling in my head; how is this possible and did he experience it too? Nobody, is going to believe me, when I inform them, I had experienced the most amazing sex ever with a soul. I was flabbergasted how surreal it felt. Though, I must say, soul sex is ten times more orgasmic than physical bodies having intercourse. The way we climaxed at the same time, left my body trembling for quite some time. During the mornings of passion, I felt the pure unconditional love, and oneness intertwine between us, which overturned the sense of separation. My heart and soul will never be the same. During this point, Daniel was sleeping in the spare room in order to give me space.

Living a Double Life

Both girls came home from college in the summer of 2016. I was living a double life; as they had no idea what was happening, and Daniel kept my situation a secret. I walked around numb as my soul wasn't present during this time; but I was adamant of persevering through it; besides, Jackson didn't have any desire to connect in the physical world. Throughout the summer, I was extremely busy working and spending time with the girls, that I finally felt some kind of relief, since I wasn't so focused on Jackson. I pushed my feelings and struggles aside, to enjoy the short time I had to spend with the girls before going back to college. They will always be my number one priority.

Questioning Deep Desires

When fall came around and the girls went back to college, I went through a major physical shift. A deep depression set in, which usually wasn't myself; as I enjoyed to love, laugh, and have a good time. I meditated every day, but couldn't get myself out of this dark hole. When I tried to analyze my thoughts, the only conclusion I suspected it could be, was empty nest syndrome. Because I already accepted my psychic abilities and double life, so, I decided to go for counseling. I was familiar with the practice and some of the therapists, since I had acquaintances that highly recommended them. I felt comfortable making my first appointment. Although, the therapist I made an appointment with; wasn't the one the therapist I thought. I guess the Universe wanted me to see this particular one instead.

During my first session, the therapist and I had an instant connection, as I sat there on her comfy couch, answering all the simple questions while she's writing the answers down. Her office felt very homey, with plants in the windowsill and a bookshelf full of books and knickknacks. I left her office feeling confident, that she'll come to the conclusion with my issue. I went back a couple weeks later, which went more in depth with my childhood. I poured my heart and soul out to her; which I'm sure I went over my hour allotment with the history I endured. I left there emotionally exhausted from crying, since I had to relive my past. Around the third and fourth session, we talked about my marriage and family life. Overall, our marriage and family life were wonderful. The girls went through changes during puberty, but nothing we couldn't handle. We raised our girls the proper way by teaching them respect and manners. When they needed punishment, they weren't spanked or beat with a belt, like I was as a child; instead, we had grounded them, or took electronic devices away for a certain amount of time. I put an end to the cycle of beating as punishment. One session, I explained to the therapist the great connection between Daniel and me; but also felt an energy shift a couple times throughout our marriage. I couldn't put my finger on it, but something was missing. A few times throughout our twenty something year marriage, I found myself enjoying and reciprocating the attention from other men. In fact, the one fight we ever had, was about me flirting with a man at one of our block parties. Whenever I addressed the issue, we would attempt to spice up our sex life for a while, thinking, maybe that was the problem. It lasted a short while, and then everything went back to normal. I ignored the feelings that arose; thinking, everyone must go through a period like this during their marriage. Whatever changes I went through, Daniel would have my back.

    Regarding our marriage, the only other topic that needed to

be addressed, was our different personalities. With him being an introvert and homebody, I felt lonely at times. I thrived being around crowds, traveling, having fun, going to gatherings or hosting them myself. Most of our marriage, I went to functions without his presence, or he would make a short appearance and then depart. He was never a crowd type of guy. Sometimes, I'd travel without him due to his devotion toward his employment. Not only was he an introvert, he let work consume his life. As we became older and the girls were grown; gradually, I noticed him changing. In his mind, work was top priority in order to provide for the family; but once he realized his mental health and family time was more important, he became relaxed and started enjoying life. Recently, we had bought a camper and talked about traveling cross-country. In order to accomplish this task, he would have to take a couple weeks off work, which would have to be a big adjustment with him. With the therapist going deeper into our personalities, she provided a questionnaire, which then we both filled out, and everything I already knew, was staring at me on paper. I always thought opposites attracted.

The rest of the therapy sessions, felt like I was the teacher, and she was the student. I asked her, "If she knew what a Twin Flame represented."

Her response was, "No." My reply was, welcome to the club, until I met mine! With this intrigued look, I proceeded to explain my Twin Flame journey from the beginning. Her mouth didn't drop to the floor, but I could tell she was astonished with all the details that was spewing out of my mouth, especially the part regarding soul sex. At that point, I thought for sure she thought I was crazy; instead, she had advised me to take a road trip and visit him. With a shocked look on my face (because that's what Daniel advised me to do), I explained to them both, that it's not that simple, if I visit, I will never return. That's how intense our soul connection was even though on the physical plane; he didn't interact with me.

My Whole World Turned Upside Down

By the end of January 2017, I walked out of my therapy session knowing what needed to be accomplished. Over the course of two years, my soul knew what was best, but with me demanding to be in control, kept me unhappy. It wasn't empty nest syndrome that was making me depressed; I had outgrown my marriage.

   I met with the councilor one more time, to address, that I will no longer need her services, since I made my decision of proceeding with a divorce. This decision was one of the most painful circumstances I had ever encountered. I never sought to break apart our beautiful family and still loved my husband; he was my best friend, but I knew deep within my soul, I needed to grow. Right before Valentine's Day is when I broke down and informed him of my decision. During that time, he was working on the grout in the sunroom that we just built; when we discussed the decision I had made. First, as his emotion appeared as disbelief, and then the devastation progressed quickly, and we both held onto each other and cried. I must have sounded like a broken record when I kept repeating myself sorry, I didn't mean for this to happen.

   As soon as he realized that I wasn't changing the decision I made, we sat down together and discussed the logistics. I had already met with an attorney beforehand, which an acquaintance recommended, because I was clueless in what's involved with divorcing. I showed my husband the paperwork she provided to me, and we both agreed to use the same lawyer. There was no point of wasting money on two lawyers when our divorce was amicable. Even though it was my decision to get the divorce, we were both hurting and wanted to make it less stressful than it already was. We had agreed that I'd keep the house, since I owned the dog business; but he could live there until he finds something intriguing to buy and accepts his offer. When everything was set in motion, our secret we held within, needed to be discussed.

Breaking News Is Emotionally Raw

Aubrey graduated from college, and was living partially at home or with her boyfriend at his apartment. We decided to tell her first, since she we present. We all were surrounded around the kitchen table, when we had enough courage to break the news. My stomach was in knots, sadness, and feeling anxious all at once. I was the villain, breaking up the family. As soon as she heard the word divorce, her face went completely blank, didn't say a word, and ran to her bedroom. Watching her face broke my heart, so I followed her to the room. I slowly opened the door, and found her lying on the bed crying. Tears started rolling down my cheeks while I watched my little girl hurting. It killed me seeing the sadness in her eyes since I changed her world forever. I tried to console her the best I could, but all she kept repeating was, 'Someday you will regret this, Mom!' I left her room feeling like the worst mom ever, as I was letting her down. The plan to tell Kinsley was going to be at the end of her college year; but she came home for the weekend, shortly after we told Aubrey. As she walked through the garage door, I noticed she was excited to be home for the weekend and to get a home cooked meal. At first, we acted normal, like nothing was different, but then I couldn't handle the charade any more. I asked her if she could take a seat for a moment because we had something important to discuss. Instantly, she thought someone passed away, but when I explained to her no, we're getting a divorce; I noticed a part of her died by the look on her face. As she sat there emotionless, trying to comprehend the change that is occurring, we surrounded her with love and reassurance that everything will be all right. She never blamed me for the decision I had made, but lost faith in true love.

When I broke the news to the rest of my family, I didn't have the best support system. The way everyone came across, I felt completely alone. My mom thought I was making the biggest mistake of my life; didn't talk to me for months, and Doreen charged over to the house, and yelled at me. Colleen didn't have an opinion, as she had kept to herself. The only family member that didn't judge or criticize me for the decision I made, was my mother-in-law. I am forever grateful for the love she had shown, through one of the toughest decisions of my life. She will always be my second mom. Leigh and Carla weren't surprised of the divorce, since I cried on their shoulders and talked openly about what's been transpiring. But when we informed other acquaintances and neighbors, they were in disbelief, since we never showed any signs of a troubled marriage.

After everyone was aware of our divorce, it still didn't seem actual, because he was residing there making dinner and alcoholic beverages, like we usually had. We were still best friends considering the circumstances, and shared over twenty-five years together. At one point, my mother-in-law moved in during the transition of selling her townhouse and finding an apartment. It might have been strange for others, but I wouldn't have it any other way. In June 2017, my husband moved into his new home and my mother-in-law into her new apartment. There was a sense of relief once they relocated, so I could start healing and begin my new chapter in life; but with a twinge of sadness, over what I left behind.

Divorce

Our divorce was finalized July 13, 2017.

A New Chapter in Life

Spiritual Growth

Beginning a new chapter, consisted of taking baby steps toward my spiritual growth and transformation. Recently, since I followed through with what was best for my soul, even if it meant hurting others; I was devastated. With the urge to heal my inner being, I began with forgiving myself and letting go of all the guilt that was buried within, regarding the divorce. It was a horrible feeling, knowing you're the one that caused the sadness and pain to others, especially my children. Sitting there quietly during meditation every day, sometimes twice a day; helped release the burden off my shoulders. Eventually, I felt a sense of peace, with the decision I had made.

Healing Process

I started reading psychic healing and spiritual growth books, which guided me into loving myself. In my mind, I always thought I did, but once I started working on my inner child, I was broken. All the pictures my mom kept of me when I was little; you could see the hurt and sadness in my eyes; smiling was non-existent. I needed to heal my inner child in order to start the process of loving myself. While I sat there in meditation style with a candle burning, I stared at one of my childhood photos. Tears poured down my cheeks, as I apologized for all the abuse she had endured; I will NEVER let anyone else hurt her again. I sat there sobbing and hugging myself, while emphasizing the unconditional love, I have for her, and how she'll never feel abandoned again. This is only the beginning of the healing process, but already, I felt an energy shift and some light starting to peak through.

During the second step process to healing my inner child, was to acknowledge and forgive my cousin's sexual abuse toward me as a little girl. I never confronted him regarding the abuse; in fact, whenever we would cross paths at family functions or funerals, I would appear like nothing happened. I accepted his friend request on Facebook. I figured, there was no harm done, since I suppressed the abuse and never looked back. There were no family gatherings scheduled for the future, so, I decided to write him a letter on Facebook messenger. My heart felt like it was pounding out of my chest before I even had one word written. While my eyes filled with tears, I started the process of acknowledging and confronting the abuser. I went into every detail of the sexual abuse like it just happened yesterday; I advised him that he was supposed to protect, not damage me. I gave him my forgiveness but informed him, I will turn him into the authorities, if any other child opens up about his sexual abuse toward them. I wasn't expecting an explanation or apology, so after I hit send, I blocked him on Facebook and never went to family functions that he might have attended. By acknowledgment and forgiveness, I felt my inner child beaming as the healing began.

The final step of healing my inner child was forgiving my dad for all the physical, mental, and sexual abuse he put upon myself and family. He was no longer living here in the physical world, so I wrote him a forgiveness letter and threw it into the fire pit. I remembered standing at his coffin, informing him, I forgave him, but now I realized, that it didn't come from the heart. During the process of writing, this time I wasn't as emotional; because I accepted years ago that he was a very sick man. Alcoholism is a disease, and unfortunately, it caused him to become mean and abusive. I'm not excusing his behavior by any means; I just accepted the fact that he was extremely ill. Although rare, there were a couple memories that I could recall when he wasn't inebriated, where he was a fun, loving father. After burning the letter, my inner child was starting to feel safe and secure.

Not long after burning the forgiveness letter, my dad came through during meditation. As soon as I heard the word "sweetheart," I knew exactly whose voice it was, and immediately started crying. He apologized repeatedly for his actions toward myself and family. This was the first time I had ever experienced the feeling of pure love, and sincerity coming directly from him.

From this point forward, I was on the path of loving myself. The love that I found within, caused my energy to shift again; this pushed me into bliss. I will always follow through with what's good for my soul, even though at times, there's lessons to be learned.

Another night, the silence became over-bearing; and I felt the need to confront Jackson regarding our connection. Jackson would not acknowledge my existence as usual, but kept in touch with Leigh. In fact, whenever Leigh and I traveled together and would post pictures on Facebook or Instagram, he would send her messages. It was irritating and hurtful at the same time. I decided to write him a letter, since I needed to release the suffocation that I had felt from our soul connection. I wasn't sure if he would even reply or not, but I had to follow through with my souls urge. My thoughts came rushing in like a raging river, so I laid it all out there without holding anything back. I started the letter out by sharing the concept of how I felt we were twin flames, and the dynamics of the duo. I then proceeded to explain how I was able to feel his emotions, listen to his thoughts, and how my gut twinged every time our souls try to interact. By the end of the letter, I described how the connection changed my life forever. It helped release anything that wasn't good for my soul, even if it meant divorcing my husband. Before signing off, I indicated the unconditional love that I will always have for him. I read it to Leigh for approval, and when she agreed it was perfect; I immediately emailed it. I waited patiently hoping for a response, but as the night progressed, I didn't receive any notification. I decided to take it upon myself to text him in order to get confirmation that he received the email. Almost immediately, he responded back to confirm that he did; but, his response to what I wrote ripped my heart into tiny little pieces. When he justified and apologized for the way he perceived the connection between us as non-soul mates; I felt our soul break into two. He was more intrigued by mediumship and wanted to discuss more about that; but I put on my running shoes and signed off on our conversation.

The next morning, I felt uneasy with how I ended our conversation, so, I sent him a text to see if he wanted to continue where we left off. He didn't respond as usual, and then, I realized he blocked my phone number and all social media. For some reason, I was still able see his Facebook music page. Even though my heart was shattered from his response and now blocked, there was still hope within that he would awaken. In my mind, how can our connection and emotions be so different? After all the visions, soul sex, telepathically talking to one another, feeling the unconditional love, and waking up every morning with that twinge in my gut letting me know we're one.

Being discarded from Jackson was one of the most heart wrenching experiences I had ever endured. Although, I have realized our souls come together in a different dimension, but here in the physical world, he pushed me into a spiritual growth. I was already going down a spiritual path; but the path went deeper into my spiritual journey. I found myself constantly revolving and releasing things that weren't good for my soul; or I was outgrowing the connections I once had whether it was friends, neighbors or personal possessions. Going through this journey, brought a sense of not belonging. I never gave it a second thought, it was me changing within, as I attributed the disconnect of others, since Daniel and I divorced. I had a sense of where I belonged, but I pushed the feelings aside, since Kinsley was in college, and there was no communication with Jackson.

Every day, I hungered for his love, and the only way to fill that void was to watch him sing live on his music page. Temporarily, listening to his beautiful voice, helped the loneliness subside. With some of the tunes he sang, I would correlate in my mind those lyrics to our relationship, desiring that he would work back to our oneness. Every so often, I would send an IM message to say hello, and of course, no response. Spring of 2018 arrived, and I had no desire to put myself out there to date. At least, that's what I thought. I was happy and content where my spiritual journey was heading and besides; I was already in a soul relationship. It's not like I could hide or push him away. Wherever I went, he followed. One evening, Leigh and I went out to dinner with a couple of male friends. The one gentleman, we were introduced to, seemed to conform well within our group of friends. It was a pleasant evening with lots of laughter and conversations throughout the night. It was getting late when all of us decided to leave the restaurant. Everyone hugged to one another, and said our goodbyes. I never had a wow moment during the entire night with our new friend, but he grew on me out and then asked me on a date a week later.

It was a warm sunny afternoon, when he arrived in his extravagant vehicle and drove to the restaurant. The outside deck was open for the season, so we ordered our alcoholic beverages along with our meal. He was easy to talk to, and I didn't feel uncomfortable the entire time. When the relationship topic was brought to the surface, I was pretty up front about how I like to go with the flow. At this point in my spiritual journey, I believed if it's meant to be, it will be. Going with the flow, maybe lasted a couple weeks between us, until we were in a full-blown relationship. I started feeling alive again, having sexual relations like teenagers in every room of the house. I overlooked how much I loved to cuddle and express my affection. After twenty-five years, my libido was back on track.

Unfortunately, the relationship became tumultuous with his behavior. He became very possessive which didn't resonate well with me. I refused to let him control my life; only then, his true colors showed and I realized he was a narcissist individual. He would change certain situations around and accuse me or others. All the fighting he caused, was never his fault. The chemistry between us was astounding, and that's why it took me so long to realize that he wasn't good for my soul. We dated for about five months when I ended our relationship completely, but departed with friendship. Even though I tried opening myself up in this past relationship, I wasn't able to love fully since my heart and soul belonged elsewhere, with Jackson.

Road Trip

On February 24, 2018, I decided to take a road trip up to Rhode Island. Jackson posted on Facebook the location and time that he would be singing that weekend, so I decided to take a big leap of faith and surprise him. I had been stuck in limbo since our first encounter, and I needed clarification of our connection. I also, wanted to inquire if he had the same visions or dreams, which I previously had between us. He had blocked me from all social media, (Except his music page) so this was the only way I could move forward. I informed Leigh about my intentions and the road trip, but no one else. She had been one of my biggest supporters from day one; since she witnessed the soul relationship transpire throughout the cruise in 2015. Leigh may not always agree with my soul urges, but realizes how essential it is to follow through with them.

It was clear skies and fairly warm outside for a February morning, so the drive went smoothly. I asked the angels to guide and protect me throughout this road trip so my stomach wasn't in knots; I felt calm and excited at the same time. I spent countless hours envisioning and playing out the scenario in my head with how the night will transpire. I was expecting reunion, with both of us going back to the hotel room. My thoughts were out of control, which caused me to daydream the entire way to Rhode Island. After arriving at the hotel, I quickly threw my belongings in the room and went outside for a stroll around town. I wanted to get familiar with the area and where he would be playing that night, so I walked down towards the wharf. I came upon a welcoming center where the ferries come in from different islands; then all of a sudden, I had a de-ja vu moment. The familiarity of this building, in which I remember standing there collecting maps, from a previous lifetime. After my WOW moment, I walked a little further and found quaint little shops and restaurants right along the water. I felt relieved as I came upon the location where he would be singing that night, so I headed back to the hotel room to get ready for a wonderful evening. The anticipation was building, while I was getting ready for the evening that I accidently put on two different shoes. I totally convinced myself that this would be the night; we would finally come together in union. Throughout all the years of running and chasing, it will finally come to an end. We would pick up where we left off. He will be electrified to see me, embrace one another, and engage in conversation in between his breaks like we had previously done during the entire cruise. Eventually, throughout the night, he'll realize that our connection never subsided, and we belong together. I departed the hotel early in order to arrive at the pub before he started setting up, so I could surprise him. It was a dark, dreary rainy night when I arrived at the restaurant, and I happened to glance over as he was retrieving equipment from the trunk of his car. I slowly walked in his direction and said hello. There was a confused look on his face, and then, he had realized it was me. After processing the surprise, I thought his eyeballs were going to fly out of their sockets. Right away, he asked me what was I doing here. I replied that I heard someone good was playing, and I wanted to watch him perform. He provided me with a friendly hug and questioned what hotel I booked. I offered to help carry some of his equipment inside, but he declined, stating it was too heavy. After the awkwardness, I proceeded inside, looked around to see where he was setting up and sat down at the bar. It was the perfect location to watch him perform. The bar area was very small and crowded since it was a Friday night. As soon as I sat down, I introduced myself to everyone, while he was setting up. At the corner of my eye, I noticed him glancing over my way with a confused look on his face. Right before he started performing, he strolled over to the bar and started introducing me to his old boss and co-workers that I had already met. But then a moment later, I over-heard him talking to himself, since no one was really listening, inquiring as to why I was there and kept repeating the same question. At that moment, I noticed he started feeling uncomfortable with my presence. After he walked back to where he was performing, I noticed him talking intently on his cell phone.

During his performance, I had everyone sitting by the bar requesting his favorite tunes, which he obliged. We were all having an amazing time, listening to his music and chatting to one another. Then out of the blue, Jackson strolled over during his break and advised me, that he was on a blind date. (Which, I assume he had arranged by the phone call made recently) I nonchalantly, informed him to have a good time, I was planning on departing, shortly. Before I had a chance to leave, he introduced me to his blind date and sat down next to me. I personally, have never been on a blind date before, but this date; brought a container of leftover food to the restaurant for his dinner. During his meal, he had ignored the woman and kept the conversation between us. By the end of his break, he informed me that he needed to focus on his date, and was no longer able to engage in conversation. I responded; not a problem, I was leaving anyway with the friends I encountered. As I stood up, his hug was nonexistent, then provided a handshake and said, "It was nice seeing you again."

I left there devastated, confused and dazed. My friends knew about the situation since we had discussed it earlier in the evening, and they tried their best to console me, even though they were on their anniversary get-away. We proceeded to another restaurant that was right around the corner, they bought me a drink; and then I let them enjoy their evening alone. I walked back to the hotel in the drizzly dark and damp night sobbing as my world was shattered. I tried calling Leigh in the middle of the night, but no answer. When I finally reached my hotel room, I passed out on the bed feeling like someone stabbed my heart into a million pieces. The next morning, I woke up hungover and mentally exhausted. The night had not planned out like I envisioned, and I did not get clarification that I desired. I was on an emotional roller coaster all the way home from sobbing, then turning to anger; especially when Leigh returned my call. Evidently, he was freaking out and texted her several times throughout the evening, wondering why I was present. My car came to a screeching halt to the driveway, because now I was livid, ran inside the house, and burned everything that pertained to him. Later that night, I lit every candle I could find, and placed them around the Jacuzzi tub. I laid in the warm bubbly water for hours, listening to guided mediation that would cut the cord between twin flames. I no longer wanted to be in a soul relationship, if we cannot be together in the physical world, as it's too painful to bear. The next morning, the meditation was ineffective, as I felt our souls interacting.

 Two days later, Leigh, who's one profession was Life Coach Councilor, received a phone call at work from a police officer, where Jackson resides. Leigh and Jackson had kept in touch on Facebook messenger since our cruise, but she was flabbergasted as to how he received her work number. The officer and Jackson were on speaker and were questioning my mental health because now, I was accused of being a stalker. The conversation between the three of them didn't go very well, as she was getting annoyed, because the officer wasn't even in the right jurisdiction, and they were interrupting her at work. Not to mention, accusing me as being a stalker because I went to hear him sing in a public restaurant. She expressed her opinion regarding this matter, and advised Jackson if he wanted to keep his performances private, he shouldn't post them on Facebook. Before the call ended, the police officer asked for my phone number. He had called multiple times and left me messages, but we kept playing phone tag. I never spoke to him directly; but I left him a message stating that Jackson can stop distressing, because I never want to see or speak to him again. After hanging up the phone, I became so furious over the charade, that I couldn't stop shaking.

Surrendered to the Universe

I was at a loss, which didn't allow me to move forward, and I couldn't handle the pain I was causing myself; so, from that point forward, I gave up all control and surrendered to the Universe. With letting them take the wheel, I sat back and enjoyed the ride. I never questioned, just followed every sign or message that I received. By doing this, I learned to accept what is, even if it meant being in a soul relationship and not expecting anything more. Going with the flow now, felt like an adventure, and I never knew what to expect next. With every new experience or lesson to learn, I trusted the Universe as it was meant to be. Again, no questions asked.

One day, I decided to go shopping at my favorite spiritual store to purchase some books. I wasn't really looking for anything in particular, so I walked around, while drinking hot tea that was offered and gazed at everything they had on their shelves. A little while later, I walked out of the store with Tarot Cards, not books. I said to myself, "Okay, Universe, I guess you want me to learn Tarot Cards." I was so excited that as soon as I arrived home, I started studying each card intently one by one. There were sixty-five cards in the deck; it took me around a month to memorize what each one represented. I signed up for an online course that taught me how to interpret the meanings of the cards, and how they are intertwined with different patterns. My favorite was the Celtic Cross, as it told a whole story from the beginning to end. First, I started practicing a three-card draw (which is past, present, and future) with my family until I felt confident. Being an empath, I noticed that I was a natural in reading energy, so I started working on the Celtic Cross, which is a ten-card draw. In the summer of 2018, I held free readings at the house and about ten people showed up. After listening to everyone's comments afterwards, I never doubted my ability or the interpretation of energy that came through the cards in each reading. I fell in love with helping others through Tarot Card readings. I created a business page and added it to Facebook. I had no expectations as I went with the flow of what the Universe had in store for me next. Leigh, who has been my sidekick for over nineteen years, has never judged or questioned any of my decisions. She only displayed love and support throughout some of the most challenging times in my life; we were inseparable, until she moved to Alabama in the fall 2018. Our paths of life seemed to run parallel with one another, which made our connection even deeper than best friends, we are soul sisters. Both of us divorced after twenty-five years of marriage, met our twin flames (she experienced a physical relationship), and went through a spiritual awakening together. Whatever roadblocks our path threw at us, we had powered through them together. Our energy connection is undeniable, and we will always have each other's back, no matter what state we reside in. After Leigh relocated, I had this knowing, that it wouldn't be long before I relocate too. Even though there was never a physical relationship with Jackson, he had pushed me into a spiritual awakening. I was releasing anything that wouldn't allow my soul to grow, in order to bring in new opportunities. Gradually, during the awakening, I sensed of not belonging in Pennsylvania, even though both of my daughters and family still resided there. I tried to ignore the yearning within, but found myself picking up the computer periodically, looking at the housing market in Narragansett, Rhode Island. I was not familiar or heard of the town, until I met Jackson who resides there. While researching, I was a little overwhelmed because of how expensive the housing market appeared. With the sale of my 2900 square foot house, wouldn't even put a dent in a mortgage payment for the exact square footage in Narragansett. As I was exploring homes in surrounding areas, I recognized that some towns close to the proximity were less expensive for more square footage, so I started looking at other options as well. Whatever the Universe had in store for me, I felt this move would happen eventually. The more I surrendered to the idea, my heart and soul opened up completely, and then I knew one hundred percent, that l belonged in Narragansett. Since I had this knowing, during casual conversations among my family and friends, I would inform them that one day, I will be relocating to Rhode Island. In my mind, the Universe would not have me relocating until after Kinsley's college graduation, in 2020.

For the first time in my life, I went through the holidays relaxed and beaming. I had a whole new outlook and faith with the Universe, so I celebrated the new year 2019, with an open mind and let the Universe take the wheel. It turned out to be, one of the most, wild roller coaster ride with all the twists and turns, but exhilarating at the same time, that I had ever experienced.

I booked an Airbnb a year in advance for the whole month of March 2020 in South Kingston, RI (only minutes from Narragansett) so I could get acquainted with the area. I spoke with the owner directly; he said dogs were permitted (which was perfect, since I owned one). Because I booked so far in advance, I would be eligible for a full refund, if I had to cancel for any reason.

As the season turned to spring, I felt the need to start fixing and updating around the home. I gradually started from the outside, painting the front door, filling in cracks to the sidewalk, clearing out the garage, and changing the mailbox. The outside of the home wasn't a challenge, but the inside consumed most of the summer months to touch up every room, update fixtures, and rummage through all the girl's belongings that were left behind or no longer needed. Aubrey didn't take completely everything when she moved in with her boyfriend, and Kinsley had an excuse since she was still in college.

The dog business was still going strong, mostly with the normal clientele. On numerous occasions throughout the summer, I would be out walking the dogs in the middle of nowhere with green grass and fields, and come across a beer can that said Narragansett Lager. With each beer can sighting, an enormous smile would come across my face. This would be a sign from the Universe, validating what I already felt in my heart; this is where I belong, Narragansett, RI. I would pick up the beer can and say thank-you, Universe. Occasionally, I would carry the beer can the entire way home and kiss it before tossing it in the trash; depending how many dogs, I was walking. These signs from the Universe, lead me to focus on contacting a realtor in Narragansett. I had no idea where to begin researching, since I didn't know a single soul, other than Jackson who thought I was crazy and a stalker. I started researching daily on Zillow, to catch any new homes that were in my price range. I came across one property that I placed in the love queue. I know for a fact, I never loved this property because the pictures didn't look familiar, and it was the most unattractive house I have ever seen. Plus, it was out of my price range. I scrolled down to the bottom of the page, and came across the realtor that was listed. Immediately, I picked-up on the sign from the Universe, and said thank you. I contacted Julia and left a voicemail, and she returned my call within twenty-four hours. Instantly, I knew why the Universe had me contact her, as we were very compatible. I explained to Julia what my thought process entailed; I would like to relocate the summer of 2020 (contingent upon selling my house). During my previous researching, I knew I had to market my house on my own in order to save on funds. Julia said perfect, as it gave her ample time to find listings that would meet all my requirements. Leigh and I were taking our annual cruise in Oct. 2019, when I received a phone call while we were waiting in the airport for our flight. It was my neighbor calling to inform me that she had a friend who is looking to purchase a home, and she instantly thought of me. My neighbor was already aware that I was planning on placing it on the market, so she asked if she could provide them with my information. I said sure, since I finished the updates and painting, where it almost looked brand new. After our conversation ended, I had a moment of panic, as a thought entered in my head, where would I relocate to, if they wanted to purchase the home immediately? I didn't even come across a home that appeals to me or could afford in Rhode Island. I quickly released all thoughts, let the Universe take the wheel, and focused on the fun vacation, we were about to embark on. After getting back from a fun-filled cruise, I received a phone call from my neighbor's friend. I scheduled an appointment for the entire family to walk through the house. When they arrived, it was a family of three, a two-year girl and a baby on the way. They appeared to be a nice couple and the house would be perfect, since they were expanding their family. We started the tour on the main floor, walked up to the second floor and then the finished basement. They absolutely loved the home with all the comments and visualizations they were discussing during the walk through. Coming to the end, I proceeded to take them outside to see the patio and the property line between both neighbors from the acre of land that I had. We stood outside for over an hour going over the history of the home, neighbors, and school district. After answering all their questions, they thanked me for showing them my beautiful home, and said they'll be in touch. That night while meditating, I thanked the Universe and said, "I'm ready for whatever happens next." Two weeks later, I received a phone call from the prospective buyers, stating they loved everything about the house, but decided, it wasn't the right time to relocate with a baby on the way.

November 5, 2019, I walked outside with the for sale by owner sign, stuck it in the front yard and started the process of advertising the 2900 square foot home on Zillow. It was a slow process listing my home, since I had to take immaculate photos of the entire house including the outside with different angles. Then, I had to enhance a description, so you could visualize as though you're actually walking through each room. I absolutely loved my four bedrooms, two and half bath, vaulted ceilings, newly octagon shaped sunroom, dining room, partially finished basement with a glass block bar, huge kitchen, utility room, and wooden floors. Now, all I needed was that one special family who would feel exactly the same. A couple of the rooms could use updates, but for, the price I advertised after researching other homes in the area, my home was well worth the money. My thoughts turned into actions pretty quickly; the house was ready to be shown. In my mind, I thought the process of selling would take longer since I prepared to be my own realtor. I immediately called my friend Lorraine, since she became a realtor, and asked if she could assist me with the contract once it's sold; she obliged. I started enjoying being a realtor, as I was receiving prospect calls, and scheduling appointments for showings, but it was exhausting, keeping it pristine, while running the dog business.

 I touched-base periodically with Julia in Narragansett, but I was also researching homes through Zillow. I came across a three-story home that caught my eye because it was completely remodeled. I thought this would be perfect because I wouldn't have to make repairs. Two days later, I was taking a road trip to Rhode Island to meet Julia for the first time and to walk around the home. After the long six-hour drive, I had arrived there before Julia, so I walked around the exterior of the house. I was pleasantly surprised how adorable it was, all nestled in a corner lot, and partially overlooking the lake. The land was smaller than I expected and the neighboring home was close proximity. Once she arrived, I felt the excitement between us, as we finally get to place a face to a voice. After her warm welcome to Rhode Island, I proceeded to follow her into the main entrance, which was the partially finished basement. As soon as she unlocked the door, I noticed a musty aroma, which I thought was strange since it was just remodeled. After walking through the entire house, I fell in love with some of the simplest details, and the total reconstruction involved with this home. The only thing I disliked, was the master bedroom, with only one window, and that was a single door leading out to a small wooden deck. Even though this home had a couple minor details that I disliked, it was precisely what I was looking for; three bedrooms, nice open design on the second floor, and plenty of windows along with sliding glass doors that lead out to wooden decks. Before heading back to Pennsylvania, Julia wrote down all my questions in order to inquire the listing agent. I walked away with putting a bid on the house. Of course, it was contingent upon selling mine and looking into all the questions I had inquired. A week later, I was having dinner with some friends, when I received a phone call from Julia stating that the owner declined my offer. She asked if I wanted to counter offer and my reply was, "No, thank you, it wasn't meant to be."

In the meantime, I scheduled showings for a possible buyer during one of my busiest days of dog sitting, since it was the only day suitable for them. I made sure they were aware of the dogs beforehand, and they said, "Sure, not a problem." Her husband happened to drive by the house and saw the sign in the yard when he was running errands for his employment. When they arrived at the front door, they were greeted immensely, with all the dog's showing affection toward their children. It was a beautiful family with two little girls.

Immediately, they reminded me of mine, when we built this home, and I believe it would be perfect for them as well. I gave them the tour; by this time, I was an expert in showings. I made sure I had all the paper work in a file from taxes to electric bills, just in case anyone enquired. The couple didn't display any emotion while viewing the home, as they just listened closely to what I had to convey. It was difficult to read their body language, whether they loved the home, except when I left them alone outside, they had walked around the back yard for almost an hour, talking among themselves. Before they departed, I invited them back the following weekend for my open house. I advertised the open house in the local newspaper and Zillow, hoping to bring in serious, prospecting buyers. I had a proud moment as I was representing myself as the realtor, while I gazed around this beautiful home Daniel and I had built for our family. I had never seen it look so pristine before, except when we first moved in. I made the open house feel homey with lighting candles that had a sweet aroma, offered red or white wine, water, chocolate chip cookies, pretzels and chips displayed on the kitchen table. I was excited when the clock turned one, when I opened the doors for all prospect buyers to gaze around my beautiful home. When an hour went by, and nobody appeared. I didn't get discouraged; I just remained at the table devouring the yummy cookies. Finally, I heard a knock on the front door and when I sprung it open, it happened to be the same family that was here a couple days ago, along with her parents. I didn't feel the need to show them around again, so they proceeded to take her parents on the tour. When the family finished viewing the inside of the home, her mother and grandchildren stayed behind eating snacks, while the rest of the family went outside and strolled around the yard. I joined her mom while we were relaxing in the living room conversing and entertaining the grandkids. Before everyone departed, I answered any questions they had, and I noticed her parents giving them their approval with purchasing the house. Before walking out the door, they advised me they will stay in touch. The open house ended, and they were the only prospects for the showing.

"The Chateau"

A couple days after the open house, for some reason, as I jumped out of bed one morning, I grabbed the computer and started researching new listings in Narragansett, Rhode Island. Sure enough, there was one that was just listed on the market. I quickly glanced at the home, but didn't have this immediate reaction where I felt the urge to call Julia. I went about the morning walking dogs and when we arrived home, I glanced at it again. It was definitely a different style home than what I was accustomed to. It almost looked like an "A" frame but had a flat roof. They listed it as a Chateau. The more I stared at the pictures and researched the property (Built in 1974 with 1700 square feet), the more I became intrigued. It was in my price range and had three bedrooms, which was a necessity, since I had two children. Within that particular day of discovering the new listing, I had a psychic reading from a gentleman in Alabama. Leigh, recommended him, and she said his readings were accurate.

When I answered the phone call, the very first thing he said was, "Why are you waiting on that house?" Then, throughout the reading, he kept reinstating that I needed to follow through with that home. I was scheduled for a half hour reading, but he went way beyond my time allotment. By the end of the conversation, Leigh was correct, he was an astounding psychic, and I called Julia to schedule a walk through.

My mom decided to join me, so we drove up to Narragansett, but unfortunately, the only time that was good for the listing agent to be present was three o'clock. He was the only one with a key to get inside the home. That didn't provide enough daylight to walk around outside, since it gets dark around four thirty. As we parked the car into the driveway, I glanced over to look at this unique home with painted blue wood shingles and yellow colored rim around the sliding glass doors. They also had matching yellow flower boxes mounted to the front of their deck. When we exited, Mom's vehicle, it was very cold with fresh snow on the ground. Apparently, Julia is always fashionably late, as I seem to arrive before her. We walked up a couple snowy covered steps until we were on the landing of the deck that wraps around most of the entire house, and noticed their above ground pool wasn't closed for the season. My mom was shocked by this neglect since she has a pool and knows that it should have been closed a couple months ago. Due to freezing temperatures, it could ruin the pump. We proceeded to walk around the perimeter of the home and notice an old dilapidated steel shed with the doors hanging by threads. I was afraid to peek inside, as it might collapse on my head. The owner's land was fairly wide, as the home was built on two separate parcels, which was partially fenced, and an old stone-wall in the back dividing the property line from the forest. The forest behind the home was considered common land and no one will be eligible to build. Even though there was light snow covering the roof, I noticed moss growing in between the shingles, more so on the one side. When both realtors arrived, we followed them inside. My mom went one way and Julia and I went the opposite. I wasn't completely impressed while walking throughout the home, because it was definitely a fixer upper. Both bathrooms needed to be gutted and remodeled, and so did the upstairs loft area since the carpet was ancient and smelled like dog urine. Most of the windows, and sliding glass entryway were the originals back in 1970s and lost their seal. It appeared as if you were staring outside to permanent fog. Both bedrooms on the first floor were in decent shape, but in need of new carpet, since there was nail polish and marker stains everywhere. The master bedroom is what caught my eye, as I was pleasantly surprised with the dimension and the beautiful view of overlooking the forest. The galley kitchen was updated with granite countertops, oak cabinets and stainless-steel appliances except the dishwasher that was falling apart. Although, Julia noticed the granite countertop wasn't level in the one corner, which could cause water damage to the cabinets below. I was writing down notes and so was Julia, as we stepped into the living room and dining area. I loved the open floor plan with windows and sliding glass doors around both rooms. You could witness the sunrise and sunset from both areas of the house. They also, had a pellet stove in the living room, which was the exact same brand that I owned. I was excited, as I already knew how to clean it properly, and it kept the house warm and cozy. Apparently, the owners didn't clean it regularly, since there was so much soot piled up, that you could barely see through the glass door. All the hardwood floors needed to be sanded and stained, since there were deep scratches embedded throughout the kitchen and living room. After Julia and I walked through each room, everyone joined together and proceeded to the finished basement. The steps were carpeted, but appeared to be dated back to when the house was built. Once I got passed the ugly steps, I was astonished to see how large the basement appeared. There was a separate entryway for the washer and dryer, and a decent size living room. When I went to glance into the closets, furnace, and the electrical box area, they were piled high, with all their belongings; you couldn't move forward with the inspection. After the tour of the basement, we quickly ran outside to look around one more time, as the sky was getting dark. Julia informed me that she will be back to inspect the entire roof once the snow melts. Before heading back to Pennsylvania, I decided to inspect the house one more time. Julia had followed, as we're comparing notes with one another as to what needed to be replaced or fixed. The owner of the house sprung the sale upon his realtor last minute while he took his family to Disney World. The home was definitely not worth the asking price; but with the owner on vacation, it provided us ample time to research the expenses to repair and replace. Only then, would provide his realtor with my proposal. There was one other thing Julia wanted to show me before departing, so I followed her two blocks down from the house, and we came upon a small beach sitting on a river, which flows out to the Atlantic Ocean. I was not familiar with the area or state, until she provided me with a geography and history lesson. Rhode Island is the smallest state in the entire United States, has 400 miles of coastlines, and Narragansett was one of the areas where Native American tribes settled. No wonder, I couldn't pronounce some of the road signs, since they represented Indian or tribal names. On the way home, my head was spinning in all kinds of directions. I wasn't thrilled with purchasing a fixer upper, but I sensed this is where I belong. A week later, Julia and I discussed and agreed, on the proposal we will be representing to the seller.

After the snow melted off the roof, she went out to inspect. She noticed the right side of the roof was decent since it was newer, but the left side was full of tiny holes. Apparently, the owner tried to pressure wash the moss off the shingles, which caused the damage. Of course, after witnessing the destruction, our offer was accurate to what the sale of the home should have been. My gut was accurate, as he declined the offer. But then, a day later, I noticed the owner raised it by ten thousand dollars on Zillow and advertised an open house. I informed Julia of the change, and she was flabbergasted. After researching, Julia advised me to release any worries because the owner previously put in a proposal for another home. Which means, he had to sell his home before the date expired with the new home proposal. I felt completely calm, while she's fighting with the listing agent; knowing damn well the owner's advertising price was astronomical. There was another sign from the Universe; Julia informed me that the open house wasn't a success, and there were no offers. While I was dealing with semantics with the house in Rhode Island, I received a phone call from the prospecting couple that were here twice. They wanted to come by again, this time with their realtor. I obliged, but reinstated that I will only sell this property on my own. When they arrived this time, it was only the gentleman and their realtor that walked around. Right before they departed my home, their realtor provided me his business card, and said we'll be in touch.

Finding Strength Within

On November 21, 2019, my house had sold, and I bought the home in Narragansett, RI! The new buyers offered more than my selling price in order to compensate for their realtor's commission, and the owner in Rhode Island reduced his price, then accepted my offer. Sales for both homes were contingent upon inspections.

Again, I wasn't planning on relocating this quickly; but I went with the flow and followed the signs from the Universe. There must be a reason why they wanted me to relocate sooner than later, it was meant to be. The roller coaster that I had been riding on will now be going even faster. The beginning of a new chapter of my life is right around the corner. I'm excited to see what the Universe has in store for me, once I get situated. I will be leaving everything behind, including my businesses, but I have total faith the Universe will provide the signs to follow with what my next journey will entail. I have this knowing, without a doubt that Narragansett is where I belong. Immediately, I had to inform the girls of the news. Aubrey lived with her boyfriend and Kinsley was in her last year of college. Both were aware of the house being on the market, but exactly like me, they hadn't expected it to happen so soon or even happen at all. With all the excitement of starting a new chapter in life helped me push away the thought of leaving my girls. They were my world, and I knew if I would have let that one thought of separation come into my heart, I would have backed out instantly with this transition. I finally broke the news to them; in my reality, I was hoping they would show the same enthusiasm that I was feeling, but instead, they were emotionless. Kinsley; even made a comment, saying she felt like a homeless person, since she won't have a place to come home to any more. Again, I kept seeing the bright light at the end of the tunnel while they processed and reacted to this change, I didn't doubt my decision. I expressed to her numerous times, that she would be all right since her dad's home is nearby. Again, I felt like I turned their world upside down, just like the divorce, but I knew, I had to follow through with what was good for my soul. I'm pretty sure at this point, my whole family thought I was insane or blamed it on menopause. They didn't verbalize it, but you could tell by their expressions. I was moving to a strange town, not knowing a single soul; except for Jackson, who pretends I don't exist. I would have thought the same thing, if I hadn't gone through a spiritual awakening. It allowed me to have complete faith, that the Universe has my back, and only wants best for my soul's growth.

    I advised my dog clients that I was relocating and possible moving date, so they can find another dog facility to love and take care of their babies. All the owners were frantic and emotional, as they didn't want me to depart the area; I was distraught too. I treated and loved each and every one of them, as if they're were my own.

I started listing my possessions on Facebook marketplace; since I had to downsize. With being solo in this process, I began packing immediately. I went to several stores to purchase packing supplies, and an acquaintance dropped off boxes from his employment. I began packing upstairs and worked my way down. Any of the girl's belongings, my mom said, I could store in their garage. My parents weren't home, since they're snowbirds, and didn't witness my transition. My home started feeling similar to an auction with people coming and going; filling their automobiles to the max. You name it, it was gone: furniture, paintings, treadmill, drums, exercise equipment, tools, outdoor furniture and fire pit. Within three weeks, I was sleeping on a single mattress on the floor. In the middle of selling my possessions, I had their inspector and buyer arrive; instantly, I sensed he was going to be difficult, and I was correct. Usually, you're away during inspections, but since I was the actual seller, I needed to be present. The adjuster picked apart every little thing regarding the house. I might have been a little biased, but my home was only twenty years old and in mint condition (except the roof needed to be replaced within five years, but the buyers were already aware of that). A week later, their realtor mailed me the list of items that needed to be addressed. All the receipts and paperwork of the repairs had to be submitted within a week before the closing date; which gave me less than a month to finish due to the holidays.

After the New Year 2020, I drove to Narragansett, Ri and met with the inspector and Julia. We thoroughly walked through each room, and then proceeded to the exterior. I focused intently to the information they said, whether it was a pass or fail situation. I wasn't shocked when they explained certain things weren't finished properly like the wiring in the outlets, or having a floating deck that isn't fastened properly. Just a few examples out of many things they pointed out to me. I know I was biased on my own home but this was totally different; since the owners took many shortcuts during renovations and didn't have the major repairs completed. I drove home exhausted, as I was thinking back to all the information that was given. Within that week, I received the inspection report; it was as thick as an encyclopedia. I scanned through it multiple times before I decided to call Julia. They confirmed the oil tank didn't pass inspection, but I needed her expertise with other major repairs through -out the house that should have to be corrected by the owner. I didn't want to come across as knit-picky, but the list was extremely long for me to decide. Neither Julia nor I trusted the owner to hire a repairman with the major issues, because we saw first-hand how he cut corners and attempted to repair himself. We came to the conclusion that I would handle everything with replacing the main things like the oil tank once I relocate. We would deduct the value of a new oil tank from the sale of the home. The owner obliged to all the stipulations I provided in order for the sale to move forward; plus, Julia had him agree to a one-year warranty.

 Julia was absolutely amazing within this part of my journey as we both guided each other throughout the process. She never quit, as we hit many roadblocks in order to get me home. Now, I understand why the Universe sent the sign to contact her. I never purchased a home on my own before, but I've learned the power of manifestation in order to create my reality. Being so busy with everything falling into place, it never crossed my mind what Jackson's reaction would be, if we ran into each other in his hometown, until one night when I was visiting Aubrey and her best friend. All together as we were discussing the relocation, Aubrey's friend unexpectedly asked for my opinion on how Jackson would react to our houses being in close proximity? I was thrown back by her question, because I had no idea where he resided. Immediately, I asked her how she knew this information. Her response was, "I thought you told me." I guess the Universe wanted me to know that we'll be living near one another. My intention to relocate wasn't for Jackson directly. I was relocating because of him. Our encounter pushed me into a spiritual awakening, which brought me home, with the guidance of the Universe. Although, once I do relocate, I would hope to form a connection, whether it was friends or otherwise. I completely blocked out Jacksons whereabouts so I could focus on what needed to be accomplished before the exciting day. The buyer's realtor for my home provided the closing date, which then Julia scheduled the home in Rhode Island the following day. I worked around the clock with getting everything in order before I finished packing. Since the closing in Rhode Island was at nine a.m., I Immediately booked a hotel twenty-five minutes outside Narragansett. That was the closest hotel that allowed dogs, seeing as I had two of them. I reserved Budget's largest U-Haul that they had available. Even though I sold almost everything, there remained plenty of possessions to transport. Moving into a home with carpeted bedrooms, I scheduled Stanley Steamer to clean them after closing. Last but not the least, I went online and filled out a change of address form with the United States Postal Service; once I hit send, that's when it started becoming reality.

 Within the process of packing and placing the boxes aside, I paused a moment to acknowledge the feeling of emptiness swarm over me. Even though the papers weren't signed yet, I already felt the loss of my family's home. Tears started streaming down my face, as I'm looking back at all the great memories from the time the children were young through adulthood in this beautiful home. Replaying the thoughts of each birthday and holiday in my mind. With recognizing and letting the emotions flow, I was able to accept the fact that I knew deep within, I needed to follow through, with my soul's desires. Every passing day became more emotional, not only for me, but also, for Aubrey. Ever since she was little, she hid her feelings well, until it was too unbearable. The last weekend of living in PA, Aubrey and her best friend invited me to a brewery in order to celebrate my new journey. They offered live music, and we ended up playing Zenga. It was a remarkable evening until we started discussing the move. Immediately Aubrey started sobbing, and before you know it, we're sobbing together to the rhythm of the music. During the tears, she expressed that she wanted me happy, but she was still confused on why I'm leaving the family behind and relocating to a strange area; just because of Jackson. We embraced each other as I reassured her, that I will come back and visit her as often as possible. Kinsley wasn't present during the emotional transition as it began after the holidays, and she had resumed college. Seeing the changes, like Aubrey had, was more heartbreaking than trying to visualize the ending. Luckily, college kept her occupied; which made it manageable to cope with the transformation and separation. The day came as my journey started turning into reality, when I arrived at Budget and picked up the U-Haul. I must have looked hilarious driving this enormous machine, since I was only 5'4 and could barely reach the pedals. Luckily, I only had to drive five miles back to the house. The next day, I started loading boxes, until I received help from family and friends with the heavier items. Everyone arrived toward late afternoon, so I ordered pizza and purchased plenty of alcohol. It was a wonderful little group that offered to lend me a hand: Aubrey, her boyfriend, Doreen, nephew and a friend. It lasted over four hours to fill the U-Haul, the bed of my truck, and Doreen's vehicle. Each vehicle was so jammed packed, that I ended up throwing my belongings away or I asked my neighbors to use their storage shed until I visit again. Aubrey's boyfriend drove and parked the U-Haul over at my mom's house for a few days, until my closing in Rhode Island.

Emotional Closing to a Beautiful Chapter

After everyone departed, I slowly walked back into an empty house that was once full of life, my one chapter in life. So many memories arose and opened the floodgates; tears stung my eyes, as I could no longer hold them back. I then proceeded to the second floor; in order to take one more glance at the rooms, that once were, my daughters. I felt my chest getting tighter, as I was sobbing to the point of hyperventilating. The visions were coming through each teardrop, as I'm reminiscing. All the laughter, crying, playtime when they were little, these bedrooms were their sacred space. Finally, I gathered my composure; as there were no more tears left to cry, I knew it was time to close this chapter. Before closing the door, I kissed the wall in the living room where the girl's senior portraits once hung, and whispered, "It's time for my new chapter to begin." I drove in silence; no music, just letting the empty pit in my stomach subside. The following afternoon the new owners scheduled their walk through, so I quickly drove over to the house in order to tidy up, since it was filthy from all the traffic in and out yesterday from packing up the vehicles. While I was backing out of the driveway one last time, my neighbor came rushing toward the truck crying, saying how much I'm going to be missed. As we're both crying, we embraced each other and said our goodbyes.

I met friends for happy hour in order to keep me occupied, while the new owners walked through the home. I knew everything would go smoothly, since the house was in pristine condition, it just felt so surreal, that I was no longer the owner. January 30, 2020, I was very emotional from the time I arrived at the office building, during closing, distributing the keys, and then my emotions became progressively worse, sobbed harder as I departed. The whole twenty minutes while going through the process, was a complete blur.

I didn't look backwards, as I entered the truck with the two dogs anxiously awaiting and headed north to the hotel, near Narragansett. While driving down the highway, my truck must have resembled The Sanford and Son. I had so much junk piled high in the bed of the truck with tarps draped over. A couple of times, I had to pull off the highway, because individuals passing by would point to the bed of the truck. The tarps were flapping, and barely hanging on by a thread so I had to adjust them multiple times throughout the six-hour drive.

We reached the hotel by early evening and found that the office was closed. When I rang the bell, the owner answered through the speaker and informed me the assigned room and the key was already laying inside on the dresser. It was a small family-owned hotel with cute little cottages spread throughout the area. When I opened the door, I was pleasantly surprised, because they provided me with a two-bedroom cottage. Of course, it was off-season, but I was amazed on the size and how adorable our room was for the evening. I opened a bottle of wine, and watched TV with the dogs. At this point, the tears moved out, and I became excited for my new chapter to begin.

HOME

January 31, 2020, I met with Julia by eight a.m. for the walk through. Everything we had listed for repairs were finished along with the receipts sitting on the kitchen counter. By nine a.m., we were in the lawyer's office signing papers and getting the keys to the new home. While sitting there patiently, I sensed a belonging come rushing through along with my heart radiating with love; I was finally home. After all the paperwork was signed, I shook everyone's hand, and said thank you before heading back to the house.

 While driving, I had an everlasting smile, as I realized how many obstacles, I had to overcome in order to be brought home. It definitely wasn't easy, but it was well worth all the ups and downs of the roller coaster ride. After arriving at the house, I unloaded the dogs and the belongings that were in the bed of the truck while waiting for Stanley Steamer and Verizon to arrive. Both were right on schedule.

 Aubrey, her boyfriend, Doreen and my brother-in-law were arriving later that afternoon with the U-Haul and whatever items that were packed in their vehicles, along with my cat. In the time being, I met with Julia and her friend for lunch, at a restaurant up the road from the house. I handed her a gift basket with all sorts of Hershey's Chocolate's, for all of her efforts during the process, and making this journey happen. While dining, they were offering me advice regarding the area and what to expect. After leaving the restaurant, I instantly felt as though, I made new friends in my hometown. A little while later, Doreen and my brother-n-law arrived at the house with the distressed cat and belongings. I made sure I had plenty of beer and wine for everyone, because the six-hour drive is very stressful going through New York and Connecticut. Once we strolled into the house, the party began with drinks in our hand, and unloading whatever belongings that were in their vehicle. A couple of hours later, Aubrey and her boyfriend arrived with the U-Haul. I felt horrible when I noticed her boyfriend getting out of the truck slowly, as if he was going to faint. His skin tone was definitely abnormal. After Aubrey parked her vehicle, she informed me that he had a high fever and chest congestion. Not once, did he ever mention his condition or complain during his entire stay. Since everyone arrived safely for this special moment, I wanted to celebrate; so, I opened a bottle of champagne, and we saluted to my new home and path of life. I ordered pizza to be delivered as we started unloading the U-Haul. I made sure the mattresses were packed at the rear of the truck, so that would be the first thing we retrieve and set up to sleep on. With Aubrey's boyfriend sick, they made a hotel reservation close by in order for him to get a good night rest. All of a sudden, there was a torrential down pour, while we were unloading the truck, which made us come to a halt around ten p.m. Aubrey and her boyfriend departed to their hotel and my brother-n-law passed out in the spare bedroom. I was running on adrenaline and Doreen never sleeps, so we ended up unloading most of the truck ourselves until the sunrise. The laughter between us; was long overdue and made our bond stronger. By the end of the night, we literally, looked like drowned rats from the pouring rain.

The next morning when the sun rose, Aubrey and her boyfriend were knocking at the front door. I was hoping to find the pots and pans last night in order to cook breakfast, but I couldn't find that one particular box; so, everyone ate cold pizza, and started drinking beer. We hustled without a break since they were traveling back home in the evening. After lunch, Aubrey's boyfriend and I returned the U-Haul while everyone else organized and put together the bedroom furniture. After our return, as I walked through the front door, I was astonished at how quickly it felt and looked homey. Once the heavy lifting was finished and placing the television on the mantel, Aubrey and her boyfriend decided to depart. His illness never subsided and it was a long drive. At that moment, before they walked out the front door, my precious little girl and I locked eyes with one another. Both of us were having the same feeling of abandonment, which caused us to cry uncontrollably. I held her tight like the day she was born and said, "No matter how far apart we are, I will always love you."

A little while later, Doreen and her husband were getting ready to depart as they were visiting friends in Connecticut. They made it into a mini vacation while assisting me. As we were saying goodbye, and embracing, the tears never came to a halt from previously, so I left them flow down my cheeks.

I will be forever grateful to my family for all the love and dedication that made the transition go smoothly. Once everyone departed, I sat in silence and took a deep breath. As I released all the excess emotions that were within, it felt as though a ton of bricks were lifted off my shoulders. Only then, an enormous smile appeared, acknowledging a proud moment of bliss. Since I was unemployed, waiting to see what the Universe had in store for me next, I had plenty of time to unbox and get organized. Once it was completely finished, I was able to relax and enjoy my new sanctuary. The energy around here, felt very sacred.

Now that I felt established, I started walking the dogs around the neighborhood and the surrounding areas. The whole vicinity felt familiar, as if I lived here before. I never got lost while adventuring about. One day while walking, curiosity killed the cat. Now that I relocated, I wondered where Jackson resided. Apparently, he was close by, according to the message I received from the Universe through my daughter's best friend. I called Leigh and discussed the urge of what I was feeling. She was curious too, so we schemed up an idea in order to find out his location. Later that day, she sent Jackson a message through Facebook, stating that she had a friend that moved into his area; if she needs any assistance, can she contact him? Without any questions asked, he responded, sure not a problem. He provided his phone number and address. Sure enough, my daughter's best friend was correct. Leigh and I compared addresses, and he only lived two miles from my home.

One night as I was watching television, another soul urge arose. This time, I made sure the message was very intriguing, so he would feel the need to respond instead of ignoring me. I sent him a message on his Facebook music page, which for some reason was never blocked. I informed him that if he ever felt the desire to get reacquainted again, notify me, because I'm in his proximity.

His response again... SILENCE

Becoming "One" with the Universe

After releasing all control and surrendering to the Universe, I became one. Surrendering doesn't mean giving up; it means you allow the Universe to guide you through your soul's growth. By letting the Universe take the wheel allowed the strength and power from within (Which, I never knew existed), to persevere through each transition during the spiritual awakening. There are no coincidences, as everything happens for a reason, while pushing me through this amazing spiritual journey, was meant to be. Experiencing every road-block throughout the path of life, guided my inner being toward growing into a brighter light. As I believe and have complete faith that the Universe only wants what's best for the soul, it allowed me to be open and vulnerable to anything thrown my way. Any mistakes I create through life, I consider them all learning experiences. Also, with any decisions I choose to follow through, I never look back with regrets.

To this day, I will always follow through with the signs and messages the Universe provides, as I have written my very first book (apparently, it's not my last), and my heart is complete with the guidance of them bringing me home, Narragansett, Rhode Island.